DREAM
elevators

books by BEVERLEY DAURIO

Hell & Other Novels

His Dogs

Internal Document

Justice

If Summer Had a Knife

Next in Line

titles edited by BEVERLEY DAURIO

The Power to Bend Spoons: Interviews with Canadian Novelists

Hard Times: New Fiction

Vivid: Stories by Five Women

Ink and Strawberries: Stories by Quebec Women

Love & Hunger: A New Fiction Anthology

DREAM
elevators

interviews with Canadian poets

edited by BEVERLEY DAURIO

THE MERCURY PRESS

The publisher gratefully acknowledges the financial assistance of the Canada Council for the Arts and the Ontario Arts Council. The publisher further acknowledges the financial support of the Government of Canada through the Book Publishing Industry Development Program (BPIDP) for our publishing activities.

Cover design by Gordon Robertson
Composition and page design by TASK
Printed and bound in Canada
Printed on acid-free paper

1 2 3 4 5   04 03 02 01 00

Canadian Cataloguing in Publication Data
Main entry under title:
Dream elevators : interviews with Canadian poets

ISBN 1-55128-71-X
1. Poets, Canadian (English) - 20th century - Interviews.* I. Daurio, Beverley, 1953-
PS8155.D74 2000   C811'.5409   C00-930748-6
PR9190.5.D74 2000

The Mercury Press
www.themercurypress.com

contents

A Prefatory Note

The interviews collected in this book cover a wide range of work from poets across the country, but this does not mean that in a book of this kind there are not, inevitably, glaring omissions. From George Bowering to John Steffler, George Elliott Clark, Richard Truhlar, bpNichol, Dorothy Livesay, Christopher Dewdney, Steven Ross Smith, Betsy Warland, Stephanie Bolster, M. Nourbese Philip, Daniel David Moses, Frank Davey, Maxine Tynes, Patrick Lane, and many, many more— including three of the interviewers herein, Lola Lemire Tostevin, Roy Miki, and Bruce Meyer— this book recognizes that it is neither representative nor comprehensive with respect to Canadian poetry. In the next volume of this series, more ground will be covered.

The earliest interview in this book is from 1977; the most recent was updated in 2000. Many of the interviews focus on individual books, and make no attempt at asking questions about an oeuvre. Yet these interviews, because of their love of the work under discussion, because of their focus and adeptness, read timelessly, and offer views into work that illuminates the writers' overall preoccupations and visions.

I thank the interviewers represented in this book; not just for their contributions to *Dream Elevators*, but for their fine, assiduous attention to the marvels and joys that made such beautiful conversations possible.

Beverley Daurio

Dire Things

Margaret Atwood interviewed by Mark Abley

Margaret Atwood's most recent novel, *Alias Grace*, won the Giller Prize, Italy's Premio Mondello Award, and was shortlisted for the Governor General's Award, the Booker, the Orange, and the International IMPAC Dublin Literary Award. Atwood is the author of many novels, books of short stories and poetry, and of the nationalist study of Canadian literature, *Survival*.

It was a cold morning in early February when I talked with Margaret Atwood over the telephone. The news of George Woodcock's death was fresh in my mind, something that explains a couple of my later questions. Atwood was just finishing the publicity chores for her tenth collection of poetry, *Morning in the Burned House* (her twelfth, if you include two volumes of *Selected Poems*). Soon she would be off to spend the rest of the winter in France.

The new book had already received sterling reviews— notably from Woodcock, in one of his last critical pieces. As he recognized, it's a startling volume, both sombre and intimate in spirit, and written with Atwood's customary stylishness. We expect nothing less of her; and she delivers.

She has also a justified reputation for eating unwary interviewers for breakfast. In *Canadian Writers at Work*, Geoff Hancock posed questions like, "What is the novel to you?" and "Do you like form?" and was rewarded with answers like, "Don't be silly." Not knowing what she had eaten that morning, I began the interview with a certain trepidation.

MARK ABLEY: On the back cover of *Morning in the Burned House,* Michael Ondaatje is quoted as saying that you "bring all the violence of mythology into the present world... She is the quiet Mata Hari, the mysterious, violent figure... who pits herself against the ordered, too-clean world like an arsonist." Is that a description in which you recognize yourself?

MARGARET ATWOOD: Well, he said that in the sixties. And it could have been a description of himself. Except that Mata Hari is female. I never comment on what other people say, because the person who should be asked is them.

ABLEY: But presumably you had the right to approve or disapprove of whatever copy goes on your own book.

ATWOOD: It's a great quote. I mean, do I go about in that way every day when I get up in the morning? No.

ABLEY: I'd be surprised if you did. But especially since the title poem deals with a burned house, and fire imagery crops up in this book and also in some of your earlier work— I love the poem "Burned Space," for example— it struck me as interesting that you should be described as an arsonist.

ATWOOD: On the other hand, an arsonist is somebody who burns other things down. Remember, when he was saying that, it was the sixties. It was a time when female poets were thought of as writing sweet poetry. My poetry is not sweet.

ABLEY: This is your first book of poems in a decade. Why such a long absence from poetry?

ATWOOD: Nobody knows.

ABLEY: Did the muse desert you or did you desert the muse?

ATWOOD: Neither one. We took a vacation.

ABLEY: How and why did the muse return, then?

ATWOOD: It's not even entirely true. I published *Good Bones*, which I would say is half prose poems, so you might say that that kind of impulse went into that kind of book. But during that time, ten years, I wrote three novels that were not short.

ABLEY: I wasn't accusing you of idleness.

ATWOOD: No, good. And a book of short stories, and another book called *Good Bones*.

ABLEY: But it does seem to happen quite often that writers who begin with poetry turn more and more to fiction as they get older.

ATWOOD: See, I didn't begin with poetry. I began with all of the things I currently write. It's just that in the early sixties, it was very difficult to get novels published, and much easier to publish poetry. And poetry was the dominant form of the sixties in Canada until probably about 1968.

I finished a novel in 1963; it never got published. I wrote another one in 1964-5 which didn't get published until 1969.

ABLEY: So there's a novel, written before *The Edible Woman*, that's in a desk drawer somewhere?

ATWOOD: Yeah.

ABLEY: Is it going to be published after you die?

ATWOOD: I don't know— that's very morbid! It's not going to be published while I'm alive, let's put it that way.

ABLEY: Even so, there was a burst of lyric activity which in retrospect looks fairly astonishing: in the late sixties and early seventies, you published five books of poetry in six years, and had a *Selected Poems* by the time you were thirty-seven.

ATWOOD: That was when I had a day job. By which I mean it was almost impossible to write novels.

ABLEY: So having the freedom now to write novels means you don't write so much poetry.

ATWOOD: Well, then, why did I write this book? No, there doesn't seem to be any hard-and-fast cause and effect. I think you get to the point with a form when you've really exhausted the possibilities for yourself and for that time. Later on, you may have something else that you wish to do with it.

ABLEY: The twelve poems in Section IV of this book, about your father's death: when were they written?

ATWOOD: They were written fairly recently.

ABLEY: Did your father die last year?

ATWOOD: No, two years ago.

ABLEY: I was very interested in those poems partly because my own father died of cancer in palliative care last December. So I felt very much as if I was reading some of my own experience there.

ATWOOD: You may not actually write any poetry about it for a while.

ABLEY: Did you keep notes at the time?

ATWOOD: No, no, of course not. I wasn't thinking of such a thing at the time. I don't think writers in general go through life having experiences and keeping notes at the same time, although there is a wonderful novel by Brian Moore in which a character stands at his mother's grave as she's being buried, and is keeping notes in his head. But that's a sign that he's sold his soul to the devil.

ABLEY: Well, what would you say of me if I told you that I was keeping some kind of journal through the last months? I found it a way to keep hold of my sanity.

ATWOOD: A journal is very different from keeping notes with an eye to future work. Do you know what I mean? A journal is for yourself.

ABLEY: In Graham Greene's memoir *Ways of Escape*, he talks about respecting "the copyright on other people's lives." I think you've done that in the past: when you've written about other people, there's usually been a kind of obliqueness; you've gone at things from a tangent. But in these wonderful poems about your father's dying, there's very little of that. Your mother is a character, your sister, your brother, yourself, your father most of all. Did you show the poems to your family before you published them?

ATWOOD: No. No, I never do.

ABLEY: Were you at all afraid that your mother or anyone else in your family might be offended by them?

ATWOOD: That is the risk you take with every word you write: that somebody may be offended. And it's not confined to your family. You get letters from people you've never met, who think they're in your books. They aren't. But they believe so. And you get other people who are convinced that Character A is them, whereas in fact it's no such thing. People read in a lot.

ABLEY: But when your daughter was very young, you wrote about her quite a lot—

ATWOOD: — Not very much, a couple of poems.

ABLEY: Several poems. And now that she's grown up—

ATWOOD: — But what is the question? What people can write about?

ABLEY: The question is whether there's a copyright on other people's lives that in some way, as a poet, you respect.

ATWOOD: I think there's a copyright on other people's stories. Marian

Engel used to say, "I'm telling you this but it's copyright." [Laughing] What she meant was, "I want to use it myself."

If you're writing science fiction set on the planet Mars, you are not presumably overlapping with anything that exists in the world that you also live in. But if you're writing something other than science fiction, you are inevitably going to do that. And that is just one of the things you have to accept as a writer.

ABLEY: Sure. This will be my last question on the subject, I promise. I still can't help wondering whether there's any difference for you when you write about Cressida or Ava Gardner or Helen of Troy, who can't answer back, as opposed to when you write about members of your family.

ATWOOD: You think those people really are Ava Gardner and Cressida and Helen of Troy?

ABLEY: Maybe those readers have good reason to write to you, then.

ATWOOD: When you write a poem, and the reader reads it, the reader is not reading about you. The reader is reading about himself. It's what you just said to me: "I thought I was reading my own experience." And the reason is that they don't know you, and they don't know any of the people you know, but they do know their own lives. So of course they make connections with their own lives and not yours.

There is a kind of voyeurism— people want to know, "Is there a real cat? Was there a real house that burned down?" For the poem, it makes no difference. It's an added thing that we know. And that's why we read biographies: because we're snoopy. The last word on that surely has to be Janet Malcolm's book *The Silent Woman*, that goes into all the snoopy and voyeuristic urges that people have, both when they write biography and when they read it.

And we all have those. That's why the *National Enquirer* is so popular. We like to feel we're snooping on other people's lives, and have got the real truth. But for the poem as a poem, or for the novel as novel, it's immaterial. The thing either convinces on its own merits or it doesn't. And it may add something in an extra dimension to know that Mr. Rochester was really so-and-so. But it doesn't add anything to the novel.

ABLEY: Thank you.

ATWOOD: Do you understand what I mean?

ABLEY: Yes, and I still think you're being somewhat evasive.

ATWOOD: Well, what exactly are you asking?

ABLEY: The voyeurism is something that you address in the poem "Manet's Olympia." But I still would say that there's a difference in kind between writing about a painting or a movie star or a lion-headed goddess of war and writing about one's own family.

ATWOOD: There may be a difference of kind, but it's not going to make the poems better or worse.

ABLEY: I agree.

ATWOOD: So it's really a biographical question. Do you want to wring some feeling from me? Do you want to get me to express emotion? Is that what you have in mind?

ABLEY: No, not at all.

ATWOOD: Okay.

ABLEY: Let me ask you about a remark you made on *Morningside* the other day on, as far as I can see, very little evidence whatever: that poetry is coming back into favour, that it had a down period in the eighties but now it's coming back. Why do you say that?

ATWOOD: I talked to Mr. Book City yesterday. He said that that's right: his sales of poetry have been going up. Now you can call him and interview him— that's what he told me. He may just have been trying to make me feel good. But it seems to be the case that, although it may be up from a very small number— books of poetry aren't suddenly selling 20,000 copies— it's going up from where it was in, say, 1987.

ABLEY: I've read in other interviews that you get quite bored and annoyed when people ask you who are the writers you most admire, so I won't ask you that, but—

ATWOOD: — No, I don't get bored and annoyed. It goes like this: if I say a living person, the others all hear about it. And then they get mad, and they say, "Why didn't you mention me?" It's the same thing with, "What is your favourite book?" You name a few and then, "Well, why didn't you mention mine?"

ABLEY: The question I was going to ask was, "What are the qualities you look for and admire?"

ATWOOD: That's a much better question. In poetry or novels?

ABLEY: In poetry.

ATWOOD: I like to be surprised. And I can be surprised in many ways: I can be surprised by the way somebody has put words together, or I can be surprised at the subject matter, or I can be surprised at the way the poem moves and how it resolves, where it begins and where it comes out.

ABLEY: So the linguistic pleasure comes first and foremost?

ATWOOD: No, the surprise can be other than linguistic. I can be surprised by somebody tackling a subject that you don't expect to see, or I can be surprised by a poem moving along in a way that you think you recognize, and then all of a sudden it turns and doesn't say what you thought it was going to. That's not linguistic, exactly, it's emotional or narrative surprise.

ABLEY: I know that your fiction is much read and taught in many countries. Is that also true of your poetry? Does the poetry seem to travel as well as the fiction?

ATWOOD: No, it doesn't travel as well, and I think the reason is that it's almost impossible to translate. You can make an approximation, and you can make a good poem in another language that is based on the original. But it's so much harder to translate than prose is. And the discouraging thing is that mediocre prose is easier to translate than very good, highly charged prose. The reason for both these things is that poetry is very language-dependent, and so is, say, *Finnegans Wake*.

ABLEY: Do you ever work with the people who translate your poetry into French or German or any other language?

ATWOOD: Yes, I do. I have done. With some languages it's really impossible because you don't know them. But you will get lists of questions from the translator saying "Does it mean this?" or "Does it mean that?" They've looked up the word in the dictionary, it has in English about four different meanings, and of course when you put the word there in the poem you intended all four. And they can only have one. So they say, "If we're only going to have one, which one should it be?"

ABLEY: And do you answer a question like that?

ATWOOD: Of course, yeah, we have long discussions about it. Why something goes into French and why something else doesn't. *Good Bones* is just being translated, and "good bones" doesn't translate into French, it means nothing. So we settled on a different title for the book, which is based on a different piece in the book.

ABLEY: What's the title going to be?

ATWOOD: *The Third Hand*. Which is fine in French.

ABLEY: Even within the English language, I sometimes wonder whether poetry is often specific just to one people or one country. Les

A. Murray has a huge reputation in Australia, and as someone who's not Australian I'm not entirely sure why. I could never convince my English friends that Al Purdy was much of a poet, and by the same token a lot of the poets I know don't see that there's anything to Philip Larkin. Whereas having lived in England, I can understand. So I'm just wondering whether, even within English, poetry is almost inevitably going to have a restricted audience.

ATWOOD: It doesn't travel well. You're quite right. It's partly a matter of national concerns, or even local concerns, and landscape. I think it's very hard to understand Al Purdy unless you've gone across Canada. There's a different relation of individual to space, there's a different relation of individual to history, and there's certainly a different rhythm.

You will find that people in England often just don't get the rhyme of what you've written. I can sell a certain number of books of poetry in England because I'm known as a novelist. But if I were not known as a novelist, I would not be able to. I have managed— I shouldn't say "I," luck has something to do with it, because one of the people at Virago is Canadian— but Virago is bringing out a Gwen MacEwen book. But they didn't while she was alive.

ABLEY: Your poem "Marsh Languages" speaks of English, at least implicitly, as "the language of hard nouns,/the language of metal,/the language of either/or,/the one language that has eaten all the others."

ATWOOD: I don't think I was necessarily speaking about English. I think it's the language of technology.

ABLEY: English is very often the language of technology.

ATWOOD: That's true, but you can't put an equal sign between them. The language of Tennyson is not the language of technology. In fact the language of technology is some other language that few speakers of English understand themselves. I think there are now a number of languages that look like English but that the ordinary English-speaker would not be able to understand at all.

ABLEY: You mean the Creoles, for instance?

ATWOOD: No, I mean languages pertaining to the Internet— that whole sub-language that's grown up. I read a physics paper by my nephew, which was written in English, and I could not understand one word of it. It was completely opaque, because they're using English words to signify concepts that the ordinary non-physics person simply does not understand.

ABLEY: I guess from one point of view that's quite scary, and from another it's interesting.

ATWOOD: When bodies of knowledge develop that need specific vocabularies, those vocabularies arise. They're often made out of pre-existing vocabularies, which is why every language is so riddled with concealed metaphors. But they are not understandable to somebody who does not share the sacred knowledge. I look at some of these computer-oriented magazines, and I can't read them.

ABLEY: Is it partly that to speak in the language of conversation, and especially in the language of poetry, you need to think through images. And when you're writing advanced physics, or technology, you can't allow yourself to think in images, you have to think in pure abstraction.

ATWOOD: No, no, not even that. Those languages are highly metaphorical. It's just that we don't have the other term of the metaphor.

ABLEY: How can you have a metaphor with only one term?

ATWOOD: People who understand the special language have the other term. "Internet" itself is a metaphor, of course. Then go on from there, and there're all of these words that are metaphors.

ABLEY: Are you on the Internet?

ATWOOD: No, no, no, of course not! No. Why would I be on something that would allow other people to read my mail?

ABLEY: I guess because for a writer of fiction, it might be interesting to eavesdrop on all those other conversations, all those other lives.

ATWOOD: The Internet is like a great big wall that people can come in the night and write on. You never have to see anybody else. They never have to know who you are. And you can invent a completely different persona for yourself, and carry on a double or triple or quadruple life. One of the beauties of it, for certain kinds of people, is that they never have to encounter actual other people. It's a very artificial situation. It's words on a screen, but you don't have the body clues, voice clues, any of the other information that goes into making up a conversation when you're there in a room with the other person.

ABLEY: Yet there's a tremendous pressure going on, I suppose largely through the media, saying that "Unless you join the Internet, you're going to be left behind"—

ATWOOD: — Left behind where? Where is this left-behind place?

ABLEY: Oh, in the past! They say, "The Internet is the language of the future."

ATWOOD: No, I don't think the Internet is the language of the future. I think the Internet is the language of the future for a certain kind of person.

ABLEY: Thinking back for a moment then to the poet you were about thirty years ago—

ATWOOD: Before they invented computers.

ABLEY: Exactly. You actually have an electric typewriter in one of your early poems.

ATWOOD: And that was very advanced. Not many people had those.

ABLEY: Before *The Circle Game* was published, was it simply self-expression and perhaps fame you were after? Or did you want to be a kind of mouthpiece or spokesperson for anything through your writing?

ATWOOD: Now, may I ask how old you are?

ABLEY: I'm thirty-nine.

ATWOOD: [Laughing] Oh, my goodness, how young! Let's see now, when were you born?

ABLEY: '55.

ATWOOD: '55, how amazing. Well, you have really no cultural memory of what it was like in 1957. Fame was not an option, Mark. In high school we did not study any Canadian poets; we studied dead English people.

ABLEY: Yeah, but one of those dead English people, if I remember right, said "Fame is the spur." I mean if that was true for John Milton...

ATWOOD: But he lived in a country where fame was possible. It was not seen as a possibility in 1957 to become famous in Canada by writing poetry. That is the year I graduated from high school. I had read very little modern poetry of any kind. That summer I read *The Waste Land* and was completely dismayed and discouraged by it. Because if that's what they were going to study in university, I was obviously very out of my depth.

I had started writing a year before that. And when I started writing, I had no idea of fame, I had no idea of modern poetry, and I certainly did not have any idea of being a mouthpiece for anything. But you're talking about a sixteen-year-old.

ABLEY: Were there any poems or any writers who gave you the confidence to think that, "Yes, I can do this, I want to carry on?"

ATWOOD: I don't think it was even a matter of confidence. You have to realize that it was a complete blank. So you were not saying to yourself, "Gee, I wonder if I can be as good as Mr. X or Miss Y." It was just something that nobody did. You didn't have to have confidence to do it.

ABLEY: Why did you begin doing it, then?

ATWOOD: Heaven only knows! I have no idea. I started doing it, and it was much more compelling than anything else I was doing. Certainly better than Home Economics, which was my other option.

ABLEY: Can you move ahead a few years and talk a little bit about the climate in which you began to publish poetry?

ATWOOD: Well, in 1960, to publish 200 copies of a book was considered good. There were only five literary magazines in English Canada, and it was almost impossible to publish novels. But there were a lot of people around my age who were coming into it, who had begun to write. There were people on the West Coast, and people here in the coffee-shop movement; there was that kind of public reading going on. And Irving Layton had come into view, and so had Leonard Cohen. And people formed their own publishing companies. Publishing enterprises.

ABLEY: Your first book, *The Circle Game*, came out with Contact Press. It was one of those?

ATWOOD: Contact had been going for a little while. It was Raymond Souster, Irving Layton, and Louis Dudek; then one of them dropped out, and a man called Peter Miller came in. They published early George Bowering, they published the first Gwen MacEwen; they were considered the place to publish poetry. If you went on, you might end up in Ryerson Press's poetry series, or with Oxford.

ABLEY: People as young as I am— and I can't tell you what pleasure it gives me to utter those words, it feels like a decade since I said that— we often feel insanely jealous that we missed the sixties.

ATWOOD: Oh, I don't think you should. The sixties did not become the sixties, anyway, until 1967 or '68— it was the fifties till then.

ABLEY: But there must have been an air of tremendous excitement that you were, in a sense, creating a Canadian literature, in a way that for a young writer now is impossible.

ATWOOD: I don't think it should be impossible, because I think every generation has to feel that they're creating something new. We may have felt that, but it was hubris. Because there had been a Canadian literature before us. There had been quite a flourishing book-publishing industry in the twenties. Then the Depression came along, and put a lot of people out of business. Then the war came along and put even more out of business, and in the fifties it had to all be built up again. So they were really starting from scratch. We came along at the end of the fifties, and were able to build on that.

But think of the poets who were there just before me: there was P.K. Page, there was Margaret Avison (whom I reviewed as an undergraduate), and there was Irving, and Al Purdy (he wasn't publishing then, but he did in the early sixties), Alden Nowlan and James Reaney— we all knew about these people because the Gage book had come out, the A.J.M. Smith book *Canadian Poetry*, and there was a Ralph Gustafson collection. And all the young poets rushed out and read those.

ABLEY: In Toronto, were you aware at that time of what George Woodcock was doing on the West Coast with *Canadian Literature*?

ATWOOD: Yes, as soon as he started doing it, everyone knew about it. It was such a small community. And I think that's the really big difference: it was like the Internet [laughing]. Something wiggled on one side of it, and those on the other side felt the ripple.

There was *Fiddlehead* on the East Coast, *Prism* started up on the West Coast, there was *Delta* in Montreal (that was Louis Dudek's magazine), and there was the *Canadian Forum*, the virtue of which was that they would publish people whom nobody had ever heard of. That's where I first published. And there was *The Tamarack Review*, which was very prestigious, and around that time *Canadian Literature* appeared.

ABLEY: Do you think George Woodcock will be remembered mainly for what he did to encourage Canadian writing, or will people also be reading his own words in a decade or two?

ATWOOD: It depends on what they're looking at and studying. Anyone looking at Orwell has to read Woodcock's Orwell biography. He did so many things that when you say, "Will people read him?", it depends which people, and what their area of interest is. He was a very good travel writer, he wrote several important biographies, he was a very good essayist, he certainly wrote a huge amount about Canadian literature...

ABLEY: And he wanted to be remembered as a poet.

ATWOOD: Partly. Partly. I think he felt that was what people were likely to overlook. But I don't think he would have said, "Remember my poetry and forget all the rest of it."

ABLEY: Is there a book of poems, as you look back from the advanced age of fifty-five, that you feel most proud of? Or is it always the most recent?

ATWOOD: I think that's always a very tricky question. It's like, "Who's your favourite writer?" Or what my daughter used to drive me mad with, "What's your favourite colour?" Because if you would be so foolish as to answer, then she would say either, "What's your second favourite colour?"— and that would go on forever— or else, "Why?" And then you would be caught in having to explain why. The worst thing she would say was, "Which of my friends do you like best?" "Well, I like all of your friends." "But which do you like best?" "Well, how about X?" "Why don't you like the others?" So I try not to answer questions like that. Because you would say "Why?" Wouldn't you?

ABLEY: No, I wouldn't.

ATWOOD: Yes, you would, and then you would say, "Well, what's wrong with the others?"

ABLEY: Let's move along to my last question. You seemed very pleased on *Morningside* the other day when P.K. Page called *Morning in the Burned House* a "heartbreaking" book. Is that how you think of it?

ATWOOD: I don't know if it's pleasure; I told her that hers was a heart-healing book. No: again, it's impossible to comment on what other people say. Do you know what I mean?

ABLEY: To call a book "heartbreaking" suggests that there's quite a bit of pain that the author is dealing with. And I hasten to say that I'm not asking a biographical question through the back door here. I'm not asking about pain in your own life, I'm asking whether there's a sense in which less and less these days does poetry mourn. More and more does elegy seem to me the most natural mode for poetry.

ATWOOD: Elegy is a natural Canadian form. If you go back and look at it, Canadian poetry is heavily elegiac. But elegy is a celebration.

ABLEY: So "Marsh Languages" is a celebration of languages that are becoming extinct?

ATWOOD: You wouldn't bother to mourn something unless it was valuable. I can think of lots of things that you throw out every day in the garbage that you wouldn't spend a lot of tears over. But you wouldn't bother to mourn something unless it was worth celebrating.

Biographically-minded people are constantly pushing interpretation towards the inner and the personal and the subjective, but in fact a lot of what poets write about is there in the world. It's out there, not in here. Or it may be both, but it's certainly out there. So you're not writing about dire things because you happen to be oriented towards dire things; you're writing about dire things because they exist.

The Angel Has No Will

Leonard Cohen interviewed by Robert Sward

Leonard Cohen is a poet, singer-songwriter and novelist. His many albums include *Songs of Leonard Cohen, First We Take Manhatten,* and *I'm Your Man.* He is the author of many books of poetry, including *Flowers for Hitler, The Spice Box of Earth,* and most recently, *New and Selected Poems.* Cohen's novel *Beautiful Losers* is a seminal fiction in Canadian literature.

ROBERT SWARD: I've been listening to your album, *Various Positions.* Why that title?

LEONARD COHEN: When you're gathering songs together, the ones that you have and the ones that you can finish, they generally fall around a certain position: and this position seemed to me like walking, like walking around the circumference of the circle. It's the same area looked at from different positions. I like to have very neutral titles. My last album was called *Recent Songs* and that was the most perfect title I've ever come up with. But *Various Positions* is okay. My next one is going to be called *Songs in English.*

SWARD: What connections are there between *Various Positions* and *Book of Mercy,* your book of poems that was published around the same time?

COHEN: *Book of Mercy* is a secret book for me. It's something I never considered, although it has an organic place, I guess, among the things I've done. It is a book of prayer and it is a sacred kind of conversation; the songs are related, of course. Everybody's work is all of one piece, but *Book of Mercy* is somehow to one side. For me personally it's just a document, an important document. But a popular song has to move more easily, lip to lip. Songs are addressed and constructed that way.

Book of Mercy is a little book of prayer that is only valuable to someone who needs it at the time. It isn't aimed in the same way that a song is aimed.

SWARD: Yet I find it reads very much as if it were a love poem. It is a book of love... without the kinds of tensions that are in your other love poems and songs. It's very much an I-Thou relationship.

COHEN: Well, I hope it has those qualities, because if a thing doesn't have those qualities it doesn't go anywhere. It doesn't even touch yourself. But it is a particular kind of love poem. We always have someone looking over our shoulder when we write and we always have an idea of a public. But I think that in *Book of Mercy* that process was as rarefied as possible. The public almost evaporated in the construction of that book. It really was meant for people like myself who could use it at a particular time.

SWARD: Have you been surprised by the audience that it has found?

COHEN: I'm always happy that a thing finds any audience at all and I've gotten some very kind letters from people who are not readers of poetry. I've gotten letters from soldiers and people I ordinarily never hear from.

SWARD: In an early poem of yours, "Lines from My Grandfather's Journal," you write, "Even now prayer is my natural language." It strikes me that you may, to some extent, have found your natural language in *Book of Mercy*. And of course a psalm is also a song.

COHEN: I think that I was touched as a child by the music and the kind of charged speech that I heard in the synagogue, where everything was important. The absence of the casual has always attracted me. I've always considered the act of speaking in public to be very, very important and that's why I've never been terribly touched by the kind of work that is so deliberately casual, so deliberately colloquial. There are many great masters of that form, like Robert Creeley, but it isn't the sweetness for me. It isn't delicious. I always feel that the world was created through words, through speech in our tradition, and I've always seen the enormous light in charged speech, and that's what I've tried to get to. That's a hazardous position because you can get a kind of highfalutin' sound that doesn't really strike the ear very well, so it has its risks, that kind of attachment. But that is where I squarely stand.

SWARD: One sees the importance of naming in *Book of Mercy*, and you have just suggested that this is how the world came into being, through incantation, through saying and through naming.

COHEN: Yes, that's always touched me, the capacity to create the world through speech, and my world is created that way. It's only by naming the thing that it becomes a reality. A lot of people quarrel with that idea because that limits the direct perception of things. Everything is going through speech; everything is going through the idea, and a lot of people feel that things should be able to manifest before your awareness without the encumbrance of speech. I know it's a very old-fashioned idea and not popular today, but the kind of speech designed to last forever has always attracted me.

SWARD: You once said that "the angels of mercy are other people." What does that mean? And what is the relationship between angels and language?

COHEN: I don't know. One of the things I always liked about the early Beatnik poetry— Ginsberg and Kerouac and Corso— was the use of the word "angel." I never knew what they meant, except that it was a designation for a human being and that it affirmed the light in an individual. I don't know how I used the word "angel." I've forgotten exactly, but I don't think I ever got better than the way that Ginsberg and Kerouac used the word in the early '50s. I always loved reading their poems where they talked about angels. I've read a lot of things about angels. I just wrote a song with Lewis Furey called "Angel Eyes." I like it as a term of endearment: "Darling, you're an angel." I mean the fact that somebody can bring you the light, and you feel it, you feel healed or situated. And it's a migratory gift. We're all that for other people. Sometimes we are and sometimes we aren't. I know that sometimes it's just the girl who sells you cigarettes saying "have a good day" that changes the day. In that function she is an angel. An angel has no will of its own. An angel is only a messenger, only a channel. We have another kind of mythology that suggests angels act independently. But as I understand it from people who have gone into the matter, the angel actually has no will. The angel is merely a channel for the will.

SWARD: You speak about will in *Book of Mercy*. There's one psalm about the will and it seems to be a wall that prevents something happening or some opening of a channel.

COHEN: Well, we sense that there is a will that is behind all things, and we're also aware of our own will, and it's the distance between those two wills that creates the mystery that we call religion. It is the attempt to reconcile our will with another will that we can't quite put our finger on, but we feel is powerful and existent. It's the space between those two wills that creates our predicament.

SWARD: I am struck, in *Book of Mercy*, by the relative absence of will. One of course needs a thread of will to pray. One even needs a thread of will to write a psalm.

COHEN: Those are really ticklish questions. I think you put your finger on it. Somehow, in some way, we have to be a reflection of the will that is behind the whole mess. When you describe the outer husk of that will which is yours, which is your own tiny will— in all things mostly to succeed, to dominate, to influence, to be king— when that will under certain conditions destroys itself, we come into contact with another will which seems to be much more authentic. But to reach that authentic will, our little will has to undergo a lot of battering. And it's not appropriate that our little will should be destroyed too often because we need it to interact with all the other little wills. From time to time things arrange themselves in such a way that that tiny will is annihilated, and then you're thrown back into a kind of silence until you can make contact with another authentic thrust of your being. And we call that prayer when we can affirm it. It happens rarely, but it happens in *Book of Mercy*, and that's why I feel it's kind of to one side, because I don't have any ambitions towards leading a religious life or a saintly life or a life of prayer. It's not my nature. I'm out on the street hustling with all the other wills. But from time to time you're thrown back to the point where you can't locate your tiny will, where it isn't functioning, and then you're invited to find another source of energy.

SWARD: You have to rediscover the little wills in order to take up various positions again.

COHEN: Yeah, that's right. The various positions are the positions of the little will.

SWARD: Has there been another time in your work where you have discovered the will, where you have abandoned the little wills?

COHEN: Well, I think that in writing, when you're cooking as a writer, it is a destruction of the little will... you are operating on some other fuel. But there are all kinds of writing. There are people like Charles Bukowski who make that tiny will glorious, and that's a kind of writing that I like very much: a writing in which there is no reference to anything beyond the individual's own predicament, his own mess, his own struggle. We don't really live in Sunday school, and *Book of Mercy* is Sunday school. It's a good little book and it's a good little Sunday school, but it isn't something that I could honestly stand behind all the time. I certainly wouldn't want to stand behind it publicly. It is that curious thing: a private book that has a public possibility. But it's not my intention to become known as a writer of prayers.

SWARD: What is it like going from *Book of Mercy* to a tour of forty

European cities giving concerts, as you're about to do, singing songs from the new album?

COHEN: Well, it's not very different. You definitely go into a concert with a prayer on your lips. There's no question about that. I think that anything risky that you do, anything that sets you up for the possibility of humiliation like a concert does... you have to lean on something that is a little better than yourself I feel I'm always struggling with the material, whether it's a concert or a poem or a prayer or a conversation. It's very rarely that I find I'm in a condition of grace where there's a kind of flow that is natural. I don't inhabit that landscape too often.

SWARD: Do you really feel as though you're experiencing humiliation when you're out there?

COHEN: Well, I mean this in a kind of lighthearted way. When you walk on the stage and 5,000 people have paid good money to hear you, there's definitely a sense that you can blow it. The possibilities for disgrace are enormous.

SWARD: Are your audiences in Europe, where you've done many, perhaps most of your concerts in the recent past, very different ftom your audiences in North America?

COHEN: Speaking technically, like a salesman about territories, there are real differences in audiences. For instance, a Berlin audience is very different from a Viennese audience. A Berlin audience is very tough, very critical and sharp, like the edge of a crystal. You have to demonstrate the capacity to master your material, yourself, the audience. There's a certain value placed on mastery. In Vienna, there's a certain value placed on vulnerability. They like to feel you struggling. They're warm, compassionate. Of course it changes with seasons, whether you're playing in winter or summer, there's a thousand variables, but at the bottom, if you can find the door into the song... You're singing the same songs every night and it's necessary to find the entrance into the song, and that always changes, and sometimes you betray yourself in a song. You try to sing it the way you did the night before and people can feel it. People can feel that you haven't found your way into it. If you find your way into it, people repond to that. If you don't, you feel a certain frisson of alienation that you yourself have created. It's in the air.

SWARD: A resentment?

COHEN: It can go from a certain absence of warmth in the applause to things being thrown on the stage.

SWARD: Did that ever happen?

COHEN: I think I was shot at once at a big festival in Aix-en-Provence. That was when the Maoists were very powerful in France and they resented the fact that they actually had to buy a ticket. A lot of them broke down the fence and came into the concert and I did notice one of the lights on the stage go out after a kind of crack that sounded like a gunshot. I don't know. But they're tough critics, the Maoists.

SWARD: What about the French generally? You have said you are French. How do they respond to you?

COHEN: My work has been well received in France. One of the reasons is that they have a tradition that my work fits into. They like to hear that battle in the voice. They want to hear the real story. The well-known ones are Brassaens and Brel, but they have hundreds of such singers. They don't have a preconception of what the voice should be. So my songs have struck home there.

SWARD: There was a lot of ferment in Montreal in the late 1940s and early '50s, a lot of excitement around poetry and figures like Irving Layton and Louis Dudek. Did that touch you at all?

COHEN: Oh, very much so. Both those men were very kind to me. I studied with Louis Dudek at McGill University and he, as many people have mentioned, is a really magnificent teacher. He gave a sort of dignity, an importance, to the whole enterprise of writing that enflamed young people. You wanted to write. You wanted to be a poet. And he looked at your poems and spoke about them and criticized them in a very accurate and compassionate way, which is his style. I never studied with Irving Layton. I never felt influenced by Irving or Louis as models, and there was never any attempt by Irving or Louis to influence their students toward a certain kind of writing. But they enlightened the whole process.

SWARD: I'm sure you're familiar with Irving's assessment of you as the high priest of poetry, himself [Irving Layton] as the prophet, and A.M. Klein as the archivist. How do you feel about that?

COHEN: I don't know what "archivist" means.

SWARD: Collector of the archives. Keeper of the scrolls. Keeper of the tradition.

COHEN: Well, I would never quarrel with that. That's a useful description. Irving, as the prophet, and probably the best writer we've ever produced in this country, does stand on a mountain. I inhabit a different kind of landscape.

SWARD: Is there any tension between your role as solitary poet, if one can call it that, and the role of public performer?

COHEN: I never think of myself as a solitary poet. I don't feel any conflicts in what I do. There are economic pressures, and there's a desire, too, as a musician would say, to "keep your chops up," to keep singing and keep playing, just because that's the thing you know how to do. So between that and the need to make a living, you find yourself putting a tour together. What the real high calling behind any life is very difficult for me to determine. It goes all the way from thinking that nothing any of us does is terribly important, to feeling that every person has a divine spark and is here to fulfil a special mission. So between those two positions, there's lots of space. But I've put out a record and I know I have to go on a tour or nobody will know about the record and if nobody knows about the record, it defeats the idea of the song moving from lip to lip, and it also makes it impossible for me to support my family. So all these things conspire to place me on a stage and hopefully be able to entertain people for an evening.

SWARD: So there are really very practical considerations as well.

COHEN: Well, I don't think there is any other consideration but practical. I've never been able to dissociate the spiritual from the practical. I think that what we call the spirit or spirituality is the most intense form of the practical. I think you have to find those sources within yourself or there is no movement, there is no life to be led. Many people have different ways of locating that source. Some people avail themselves of the traditional ways which we call religion or religious practice. There are many people who have absolutely no need of those particular references, but it doesn't mean that their lives are any less spiritual. On the contrary, it might meant that their lives are more spiritual. They are living spirits. And there's no distance.

SWARD: It strikes me that there's sometimes more irony in your songs than in your poems. I'm thinking of lines like "He was just some Joseph looking for a manger." The inflections in your singing voice convey a variety of different attitudes, and in some instances an attitude like irony comes through more clearly in the songs.

COHEN: Yeah, I see what you mean. I think of Bob Dylan, who gets the inflections of street talk, the inflections of conversation, and does that with such mastery... where you can hear a little tough guy talking. You can hear somebody praying. You can hear somebody asking. You can hear somebody coming onto you. When you're composing that material and you know that it's going to occupy aural space, you can compose it with those inflections in mind. And of course it does invite irony because that irony can be conveyed with the voice alone whereas on the page you generally have to have a larger construction around the irony for it to come through. You can't just write, "What's it to ya?" If you sing, "What's it to ya?" to some nice chords it really does sound like, "Well, what's it to yah, baby?" But just to see it written, it would need a location.

SWARD: How much connection do you feel with Dylan's music, or with others, like Joni Mitchell, for example? Whose music is closest to you now...?

COHEN: Well, like the Talmud says, there's good wine in every generation. We have a particular feeling for the music of our own generation and usually the songs we courted to are the songs that stay with us all our life as being the heavy ones. The singers of my own period, Joni Mitchell, Bob Dylan, Joan Baez, Ray Charles, all those singers have crossed over the generations. But we have a special kind of feeling for the singers that we used to make love to.

Nothing Better Than Poetry?

Lorna Crozier interviewed by Bruce Meyer & Brian O'Riordan

Lorna Crozier's work has won many awards, including the Governor General's Award, the Pat Lowther Award, and the CBC Literary Competition. She was born in Swift Current, Saskatchewan. After careers as a high school teacher, a guidance counsellor, a writer-in-residence, and government worker, she now teaches at the University of Saskatchewan in Saskatoon. Her works include *Inside the Sky* (1976), *Crow's Black Joy* (1978), *Humans and Other Beasts* (1980), *No Longer Two People* (1981, which she co-wrote with Patrick Lane with whom she lives), *The Weather* (1984), *The Garden Going on without Us* (1987), and *Angels of Flesh, Angels of Silence* (1988), *Everything Arrives at the Light* (1995), and most recently, *What the Living Won't Let Go* (1999). She teaches at the University of Victoria.

BRUCE MEYER & BRIAN O'RIORDAN: There's a sort of metaphysical mathematics to your poems, a sense of all the images adding up, but not to what you'd expect them to add up to. Are you striving for this in your poems, such as in "Forms of Innocence" or "The Horizon Is a Line?"

LORNA CROZIER: Nothing seems deliberate when I begin a poem, because I have no idea at all where it is going to end up or even what I want to write about until it is already written. It's only in the revision process that I try to hone the images and take advantage of what is recurring and overlapping. I'm glad you said they add up to something you don't expect, because otherwise they'd be quite boring, to me as well as you.

MEYER & O'RIORDAN: So you are just as surprised at what they add up to as the reader.

CROZIER: I find it interesting to see where I've ended up. Favourite poems of mine are ones in which I give a bizarre or unexpected slant to things. I don't think in terms of metaphysical conceits, but the poems that work best for me are the ones where cabbages become turtles, and when the ordinary object becomes magical or different or unusual.

MEYER & O'RIORDAN: A metamorphosis?

CROZIER: Yeah. And yet I hope I am being true to the object itself, like a carrot isn't a turtle but a cabbage is— a correspondence of shape and pattern— and it is as much a turtle as it is a cabbage. I want to *see* clearly rather than impose my view. I want to be true to the qualities, the characteristics of things and the essence of things in that metamorphosis. The poems that please me the most are the ones where I've looked at something and seen it in a way I don't think it has been seen before.

MEYER & O'RIORDAN: It's not so much making direct connections with something else, it's a leap in imagination.

CROZIER: That's what excites me. It's what excited me about Neruda's "Ode to Socks," which is one of my favourite poems. The conceit in that poem is taken all the way from a simple pair of wool socks to firemen to all those wonderful bizarre comparisons that he *discovered*; a matter of seeing what's there rather than simply putting something there.

MEYER & O'RIORDAN: In your poem, "The Photograph I Keep of Them," one is reminded of Atwood's "This is a Photograph of Me." Is that a deliberate connection you want us to make?

CROZIER: The photo that I describe is one that I actually have on my desk. I suppose the mythology present is that of the Depression, the Dirty

Thirties. Although I wasn't born then, I grew up with stories about that time. Every time I'd complain about something, I'd be told, "You should have grown up during the Depression— we only had flour sacks for pyjamas and we got one orange for Christmas." In every photograph my parents have of the 1930s, my parents are always posing in front of cars. The metaphoric possibilities of that are splendid. In the past, at least, people born on the prairies wanted to get out. People like Mandel, Kroetsch, Laurence, and Ross certainly left. That is what I am saying in the last two lines of the poem: "They have left the farm,/they are going somewhere." The somewhere my parents went was only thirty miles away from where they grew up, but they did leave. They went to the nearest small city; they left the desolation and isolation of farm life as they knew it.

MEYER & O'RIORDAN: Although you did not grow up on a farm, you keep writing about farms.

CROZIER: I think I tend to mythologize the farm because I didn't grow up there. I grew up in what we called a "city," although there were only 15,000 people, but I used to visit my grandparents' farm on Sundays. My grandmother would kill chickens and pluck them. I think my fascination with animals of all sorts is a city person's fascination. I don't have the practical view of animals that a person who has grown up on a farm has.

MEYER & O'RIORDAN: Do you have a more exotic view?

CROZIER: Yes. I have a poem in my new manuscript about cleaning chickens. I remember when I'd show up on the farm on Sundays with my parents, I'd ask my aunts if I could clean the chicken and pull out all the guts. And everyone would say "Sure!" I couldn't understand why they didn't want to do it, because I thought it was the most interesting thing. I thought people should fight over this privilege. It was fascinating to see the gravel in the gizzard, and the little transparent eggs that came out in a string and looked like moonstones. So, I had the city person's fascination with the farm and the privilege of being able to visit a farm occasionally to fulfill those urban fantasies. It's interesting that some people think I grew up on a farm. The farm is never a real place for me— it's an imagined place. It's funny, when Patrick and I were first together we'd be driving through the country and Patrick would ask, "What's that crop over there?" I'd say, "That's Durham wheat," or "That's barley." About a year ago he asked me what something was and I said, "Pat, I haven't got a clue. All these years you've been asking me that and all I know are the names, *barley, rye* and *Durham wheat!*" [Laughter] He believed me and assumed because I'd grown up in Saskatchewan I knew the names of all these crops.

MEYER & O'RIORDAN: You could tell him that that's Shreddies growing over there... [Laughter]

CROZIER: And that's Cornflakes over there! [Laughter]

MEYER & O'RIORDAN: How did you meet Patrick Lane?

CROZIER: I was teaching in Swift Current at the time and he came to give a poetry workshop in Regina and I drove in for it. I was familiar with his work. Robert Currie gave me copy of Patrick's book *Beware the Months of Fire* because he claimed that we both had a similar sensibility. I must admit that when I looked at the picture on the back of the book, I thought he was a fat old man. I went in with my poems, and we met each other and chemistry happened. He was living with a woman and had two kids, and I was married and we sort of drifted away and looked at each other out of the corners of our eyes. Then two years later we met again at a Saskatchewan Writers' Guild Conference. We saw each other's names on the program and both of us knew something was going to happen. I knew I was going to meet one of my destinies and he knew he was, too! [Laughter] About two months later we just ran off together. He got in his car in British Columbia, picked me up in Saskatchewan, and we just buggered off. I wrote a note to my husband and said I'm on my way to Toronto with another poet and said goodbye. We went to

Toronto and I met, for the first time, people like Al Purdy and Joe Rosenblatt, who had just been names in a book. We began our relationship by staying in Joe Rosenblatt's house in Toronto— a weird beginning!

MEYER & O'RIORDAN: How did *No Longer Two People* come about?

CROZIER: Patrick and I had been together about two months and we were living in Winnipeg where he was the writer-in-residence. We had had an argument about something and I wrote the first poem in the sequence and showed it to him. He said he wasn't going to let me get away with that and replied by writing a poem in response. Then we thought, this could be fun, why don't we just continue and bounce one poem off another. We were both reading Jung at the time. All that summer, on the way to Winnipeg from Toronto, we had been talking about male and the female voices in poetry and wondering whether there was a difference or not. We had hoped the sequence would be mytho-logical and personal and give us some answers to the question of voice and gender, but nobody read it that way. [Laughter]

MEYER & O'RIORDAN: Could you comment on that? The critical reaction was overpoweringly negative.

CROZIER: It was. It was how dare these people air their soiled sheets in public! It surprised both of us. We had chosen the title from a Picasso quote, in which he more or less said, these are no longer two people but forms, vibrations, and colours. People didn't realize that from the title. They thought we meant we were one person joined in holy *un*matri-mony.

MEYER & O'RIORDAN: So the title is meant to be read ironically, then.

CROZIER: Yes. That's what we had hoped but people took it at face value and didn't sense the irony. I remember after it came out we read it in Winnipeg and someone came up to us afterwards and asked how we could stand in front of an audience and take our clothes off like that. The funny thing is that it has come into its own again. Ten years after its publication, it's getting positive critical reactions from people like Fred Wah.

MEYER & O'RIORDAN: Returning to what you were saying a minute ago about the 1930s— the Depression and the Crash are almost missing events in Canadian literature. Why do you think this is so?

CROZIER: Well, except for Sinclair Ross, W.O. Mitchell, Margaret Laurence in *The Stone Angel*.

MEYER & O'RIORDAN: And Hugh MacLennan and Barry Broadfoot.

CROZIER: Yes. Sinclair Ross was central to me and my literary imagination because his stories were the first things I read and identified with. His stories were like my parents' stories; Ross lived for some time in southwest Saskatchewan where I'm from. The wind he wrote about is the same wind. The false fronts on the stores and the closed nature of small-town society were things I saw every day around me, and seeing those things in a "work of literature" made me realize that I could be a writer. It was the same with Margaret Laurence. It is interesting that a generation apart, the same book was the signal work for us, perhaps because the Depression is such a central myth in the west— my family talked about the '30s all the time. As you say, considering its importance, it hasn't really worked its way into the writing as much as one would think, especially in eastern Canada.

MEYER & O'RIORDAN: Is it because the Depression is almost an issue too painful to confront, in comparison to other issues in our history?

CROZIER: Well, it affected Saskatchewan more than any other province because we had the drought along with the stock market crash. Right now, history seems to be repeating itself because we're in the middle of another drought and another economic slump. Everyone in Saskatchewan has embedded in them that fear of drought and of the Depression, and the knowledge that it is coming again.

MEYER & O'RIORDAN: You have said poetry was an "out" for you, "a way of escaping from the kind of life you saw around you." Could you elaborate?

CROZIER: I'm the only person from my family who has ever gone to university, and that includes a long line of cousins. Who was it who said that the two ways of getting out of the lower class are either through sports or art? I think it was Hugh Garner. Definitely, I'm a working class kid from a working class background. Writing to escape wasn't a conscious decision, but it was a way to enter a world I knew nothing about— it had nothing to do with the world I came from. My parents' house wasn't full of books and we certainly did not discuss literature. Patrick asks, "Did you read Winnie the Pooh as a kid?" and I say, "No," and he asks if I read this or that when I was small and I say no again and he looks shocked. I really don't know why, given that background, writing became something I wanted to do. I remember going to my first library— I thought I had discovered a gold mine. Poetry is something my family doesn't understand, although they don't feel any antipathy toward it. I don't think my father has read anything I've ever written. In fact, he doesn't read at all, except for the *Swift Current Sun*. My mom is proud of me, but she doesn't understand why I write or what the poems mean, but my books are on the coffee table. And I think she enjoys seeing herself in some of the poems— or at least my version of her.

MEYER & O'RIORDAN: Do you feel you bring anything from that working class background that has been positive for your poetry?

CROZIER: I hope so. The voice in poems like "The Women Who Survive," or "My Aunt's Ghost," is the voice of a small-town, Saskatchewan working woman. The colloquial expressions are definitely from families like mine. And I hope I'm introducing a content into poetry that comes out of my particular place in the world— western, female, working class. Collectively, these qualities have not been that prevalent in our literature.

MEYER & O'RIORDAN: Do you feel it has given you more freedom with language?

CROZIER: I don't know if it has given me more freedom, but I think it has probably made me use language differently.

MEYER & O'RIORDAN: Do you feel that there is a solid tradition of working class writing in Canada with writers like Al Purdy, Joe Wallace, and Milton Acorn?

CROZIER: Yeah, but it is male, isn't it? Al Purdy, Alden Nowlan, Joe Rosenblatt, Milton Acorn, and definitely Patrick [Lane]. I can't think of any women from Purdy's and Nowlan's generation.

MEYER & O'RIORDAN: Well, what about Livesay, or is she pretend working class?

CROZIER: I think her worst poems are her working class poems. Her best are her lyrics, her love poems. Her '30s poems about the dispossessed working class, like "Day and Night" and "Call My People Home" just don't work for me. But her poems about being a woman, about aging and loving, do. Pat Lowther is probably the first Canadian woman to write out the kind of world I come from. And others, like Bronwen Wallace, wrote about it with insight and honesty.

MEYER & O'RIORDAN: A number of Saskatchewan writers, when they write about what they know, inevitably have to come to terms with the fact of *the prairie*. For example, Eli Mandel transforms *the prairie* through his "doppelganger" metaphor for being "out of place." W.O. Mitchell treats it as a metaphor for the eternal in *Who Has Seen the Wind*.

CROZIER: One thing I've never done is write about "The Prairie." I wouldn't say any of my poems are about "The Prairie." In most of my poems I use the images that surround me, and that includes the prairie, but the poems are *about* something else, like love or death or growing old. In the poems about my parents I include the particular details of the place because that's where they came from.

MEYER & O'RIORDAN: So the poems come from inside rather than outside you.

CROZIER: Both, but the outside is always filtered through my way of seeing things. I believe the landscape in my poems is more an internal landscape than an external one.

MEYER & O'RIORDAN: That's interesting because a lot of the poets who have emerged since 1970 are writing from that external world rather than the old external world of writers such as Pratt, for example. Bronwen Wallace, for instance, wrote about and from a much more internal landscape, what was going on inside her memories and her thoughts. Do you think it comes down to the fact that we've settled the landscape and now are trying to figure out what's going on inside our own heads— trying to articulate the inner experience?

CROZIER: Definitely, but also, unlike Eli Mandel, who left the prairies, I've never felt out of place here. Whenever I've read criticism of prairie literature, I'm always amazed at the assertion that it is a hostile landscape. I do not view the landscape as barren and overwhelming. I view it as very beautiful and comfortable. The landscape may seem shocking to others and they may feel out of place, but I don't... Does anyone write abut the landscape in isolation any more? I think we're beyond the new land, new language thing of our earlier literature. The fact is, we have a literature we can all feed off now, and there is no reason to keep defining the "land." We've defined and ordered it to death. Now, as writers, we have to rediscover the spiritual and magical in it. We have to save it. Our old definitions of "landscape" and the way we live in it don't work.

MEYER & O'RIORDAN: You don't see yourself as a regional writer.

CROZIER: No. I get annoyed at the phrase because I think Toronto is a region as well although no one calls it that. I think my writing comes out of the prairies. A meadowlark may find its way into my poems, but it is more than just a meadowlark. In the introduction to *The New Canadian Poets*, Dennis Lee identified a prairie school of writing which he did not put me in. He had an asterisk beside my name and noted that I had written poems which could belong to this school but that he had chosen not to include any. He chose others. I'm not even sure what this "school" is because I think the west's best writers are individual and idiosyncratic. They don't write like anyone else.

MEYER & O'RIORDAN: Since 1975, you've published seven books of poetry. Your work seems to have gone through several phases. There are more twists of thought and more of a playfulness in the diction, and more puns. What are the most marked changes that you see in your work?

CROZIER: You summed it up very well. I think I was an extremely passionate, strident writer when I began. I had a bottle full of feelings just waiting for an outlet. I'm embarrassed by a lot of those poems now when I look at them. They are very angry, very serious poems. I took myself too seriously then.

MEYER & O'RIORDAN: There are no poems like "The Sex Lives of Vegetables."

CROZIER: No, I wouldn't have been able to write poems like those back then. I think I just loosened up. [Laughter] Thank God. I still have a lot of anger that has to come out, but in more subtle ways, I hope. And over the past ten years I think I've learned a lot about diction and tone. And I've extended the range of what I write about and varied the form.

MEYER & O'RIORDAN: Such as?

CROZIER: Such as? I think I would never have written a poem in sequence in the early years. I've become more and more interested in taking more than one look at something. "The Foetus Dreams" is an example, where I give ten views of the foetus' dream. I think that is more of a postmodern view, where one tries approaching something from ten different angles and directions, from left and right and upside-down. Where does that come from? I don't know. I don't know why that developed; whether it is just maturity as a writer or as a person, I'm not sure. It just may be that I'm a much happier person now, I'm in a very happy relationship and I'm more self-confident. I think that self-confidence allows you to take more risks and to extend yourself, to try different things. For example, to be playful about sex or to be irreverent about sex is still a risky thing to do, especially if you are a woman writer. I've had people walk out of my readings— someone at Scarborough College a couple of years ago got up and left in the middle of my reading "The Sex Lives of Vegetables." I still get the occasional "hate letter" in the mail. There are still certain words that carry a powerful punch that some people don't believe belong in poems, especially poems written by a woman. It doesn't bother me much any more, well, not as much anyway, if I upset people, if I challenge them. I think you have to if you want to write well.

MEYER & O'RIORDAN: There's an aggressive tone and a playful tone about sex in some of the poems that one usually only finds in poems written by males.

CROZIER: Yes. Some critics still think it isn't a woman's place to use that stance or that language.

MEYER & O'RIORDAN: Did you mean to shock people with them?

CROZIER: No. The first time I read the vegetable poems I didn't think they'd be shocking. I thought they'd just be fun. Initially, I wondered if they were even too silly to be published because it seems to me we've been trained to take poetry very seriously. We tend to think that if we laugh at a poem, it's somehow a lesser poem. And in our country, even now, if a woman writes humourously about sex, she's morally suspect and her poems will upset a number of people who read them. I've written a new sequence that I know is going to be shocking to some people, although again, that was not my intent. I've written a series of penis poems. I showed them to Pat and he read them and laughed. He said penises should be poked fun at. All the same, I needed his assurance that I wasn't going completely off my rocker, that I was doing something that was valid.

MEYER & O'RIORDAN: While we're on the topic of sex, one theme that keeps turning up in your work is that of Leda and the Swan. It is in "Pavlova" and "Forms of Innocence." Why do you keep returning to that?

CROZIER: I come back to it in the penis sequence, too, in a poem called "Penis/Bird." The myth itself is an extremely powerful one, isn't it? A woman being raped by a big bird is both ridiculous and powerful at the same time. It really twists your imagination trying to figure out exactly what happened during the encounter. And also, no matter what other meanings we read into it, the myth is about rape. Every woman grows up with the fear of rape. You can't stand at a bus depot or walk a street or cross a park anywhere across Canada without worrying about what the guy across the street is about to do. That's part of the female psyche— that fear of rape. Then there's Yeats' brilliant poem about Leda and the Swan. It's the one I've read for years and I think it is a *tour de force*, an almost perfect poem, though as a woman reader I have difficulty with Leda's surrender. So you've got both the myth and the literary response to the myth, and then there's the very real fear every woman has of rape, another reason for the driving force behind that ancient story.

MEYER & O'RIORDAN: So you're not concerned with the rape of Leda as the indirect cause of the Trojan war, as in Yeats' poem.

CROZIER: No, I've tried to bring it down to a more common, personal level in my poem. In "Forms of Innocence," I've changed the incident from an act of rape to an act of lovemaking and located it in the back seat of a car on the prairies beside a stubble field, into the context of where I came from.

MEYER & O'RIORDAN: Dreams are another important theme in your work, the striving for another alternative reality.

CROZIER: Oh, definitely. I'm a person who is very affected by my dreams. I have dreamt that Patrick has had an affair and I've gotten out of bed and not spoken to him the whole day. [Laughter]

MEYER & O'RIORDAN: They're that real?

CROZIER: How do you tell the difference between dream and reality?... What I carry around in my head as my first memory was probably a dream. How do you know the difference between things that happen and things that don't but that you have memories of anyway?... My dreams are as important as other aspects of my life. They're as real.

MEYER & O'RIORDAN: So that would allow you to make that very imaginative leap to write something like "The Foetus Dreams."

CROZIER: The genesis of that poem came from an article I read. A scientist, using electrodes placed on the outside of a woman's belly, actually picked up the brain waves of a foetus, and he claimed those brain waves signified that the foetus was dreaming. I found that fascinating. What do you dream before you actually see anything or experience anything? How do you dream a *tree* before you've even seen a tree? In order to answer that I had to flip into Jungian psychology and the collective unconscious.

MEYER & O'RIORDAN: Robert Bly has a theory about the different types of brains— the reptile brain, the mammal brain, and the higher more developed type of brain that dreams in geometric shapes.

CROZIER: Well, I've got a salamander or lizard brain! [Laughter]

MEYER & O'RIORDAN: You've written two very strong poems about abortion. There is a real sympathy in those poems for the situation of the foetus...

CROZIER: I'm very interested in pre-natal life— in what face we wear inside our mothers, in what we become and what we leave behind at birth. But I think the worst thing that could possibly happen would be if someone from the pro-life side used "The Foetus Dreams" or any of my other poems that explore this kind of thing to say that there should be no abortions. It would be horrible because I definitely am on the pro-choice side. I am also "pro-life." That term is one of the biggest misnomers because, of course, pro-choice people also believe in life; they are *for* life. I definitely believe a woman should make the decision about whether she should have an abortion. The lines in "A Poem about Nothing," the ones about the girl jumping three storeys to abort, should suggest the terrible acts women are driven to when they cannot get a safe, legal, inexpensive abortion.

MEYER & O'RIORDAN: What are the challenges of living in a two poet household?

CROZIER: For one thing, when you live with another poet there's an understanding of why you have to write. My husband didn't understand that compulsion. Most of the poems I was working on at the time he found extremely threatening, probably rightly so. But when you live with another poet, he understands that there's a need to write about the dark things as well as the bright and happy. And he understands that poetry isn't my whole life, either. It's only a part, but it's an important part, that helps to make up what I am, the good and the bad of it. It's hard for someone who doesn't write to understand that.

MEYER & O'RIORDAN: Yes, that's like what you say in the poem "A Conclusion:" "there is nothing better/than poetry." What would be better than poetry?

CROZIER: I'm not going to answer that! [Laughter]

Choosing Control

Claire Harris interviewed by Monty Reid

Claire Harris was born in Trinidad in 1939. She has lived in Ireland, Nigeria, and Jamaica. She has worked as a teacher in Calgary since 1966. Her books include *Translation into Fiction* and *Fables from the Women's Quarters*, which won a Commonwealth Prize for poetry. In addition to her own writing, Claire Harris has been an editor with *Dandelion* and *blue buffalo*, and is actively involved with the Writers' Guild of Alberta.

MONTY REID: How did you start writing?

CLAIRE HARRIS: I had been jotting poems in the margins of books for years, but it wasn't until 1974 that I began to write. I knew then that I needed time. I took the year off and went to Nigeria.

REID: How did that help your writing?H

HARRIS: Well, serendipity— plus the shock of moving into an entirely different culture forced me to pay attention. I found, for example, that the same actions could have radically different meanings in different cultures. I'd read a lot of African writers and thought I understood, but I could be there for twenty-five years and still not understand.

REID: Does anybody ever understand another culture?

HARRIS: I doubt it.

REID: Does a culture ever understand itself?

HARRIS: I don't think it does, especially a culture as schizophrenic as ours. Africa helped me to clarify— of course, I met J.P. Clarke. He read everything I wrote.

REID: You mentioned Clarke in the early poem "seen in stormlight"'"
which is, I think, a pretty abrasive criticism of modern Lagos.

HARRIS: Lagos is an abrasive place. I happened to be there at a time
when everyone would have liked to make certain criticisms, but
couldn't.

REID: In that poem, you use slogans off walls, bumper stickers, and so
on. Is that one of the ways Africa appropriates a Western language?

HARRIS: No. That's Africa. The sentiments expressed are African, and
the slogans were often written in one of the African languages.

REID: Can you deal with Africa in English, a white language?

HARRIS: You never describe the African reality, only an English
speaker's perception of that reality, which is probably why many African
writers also write in their own languages.

REID: Is there less of a gap between literature and its audience there
than there is here, for instance?

HARRIS: I think that the reason we have the gap here is because we've
established three different kinds of poetry. There's babushka poetry,
which is not just ethnic, but justifies our current existence because of
our ethnicity, by having this grandmother who has this beautiful quilt
she made in Saskatchewan while the wind was howling and the man was
off fighting the wolves. We use that poetry in various ways and it may
have some validity, so long as we don't get entirely lost in it. Then we
have what I think has happened to most North American poetry. It's
retreated from the world. It's always struggling with its own emotions.
It's as if every time you sat down to talk to someone they told you about
their love affairs. And then there's public poetry. It's about politics and
it affects everybody. But politics is unacceptable in Canadian poetry.

REID: You surely can't blame all that on poets. Even if poets were
writing as politicized a poetry as they could, there would still be an

immense public out there that wouldn't be interested. The public itself is depoliticized.

HARRIS: That's true, this is not Eastern Europe. In a democratic society people don't need codes, and there is television. But it's a matter of degree. I think that in Western Canada people feel colonized, they sense a lack of control. Entertainment, fashion, ideas, everything seems to come from somewhere else. That leaves money. So conspicuous consumption becomes a kind of art.

REID: Why do you say Western Canada?

HARRIS: Perhaps I should say Alberta. My theory is that most other societies value both local cultural tradition and the art. I think that here the local tradition is nurtured. But the arts are viewed with suspicion. Of course, most people out here have lost their original language. Perhaps subconsciously, they feel that English and all its aberrations has nothing to do with them. It's nice to be in on the beginning of things, but it would be nice to follow along behind, too. I think that kind of alienation is more characteristic of Alberta.

REID: Wouldn't you associate that with major centres of power?

HARRIS: Okay, look at the U.S. All those guys, the whiskey kinds, the land grabbers, the robber barons— in order to gain respectability, they set up foundations. And regardless of where the money originally came from, they now support the arts. Where are our foundations?

REID: But it doesn't mean anything. The poet is still powerless.

HARRIS: True— only a writer's power comes from his ideas, and the fact of support makes it possible to write.

REID: But isn't that work marginalized? It just becomes another form of accommodation. We'll let you in because, in fact, you're not going to say anything important.

HARRIS: But if you do you end up on the cover of *Time*, like Forché.

REID: That's a pretty rare occurrence. And for all its power, Forché's book distances events. It's another revolution in a sweaty third-world country. Somehow it's kept apart from our lives. And it's possible such books just legitimize that distance.

HARRIS: That's another interview. I still think it's worse out here in the west because there is relatively little support. Even if you refuse to be marginalized at least in your own mind, you are marginalized because you can't stay at home and write. At least I won't be able to, in my lifetime.

REID: Are you uncomfortable with being a part-time writer?

HARRIS: I am. I think the reason for this is because I write in spurts. It only happens three or four times a year, but when it does, it's like a disease.

REID: How long does it happen for?

HARRIS: Well, I've been going through a really bad three weeks. That's usually about the length of time. I'll probably dry up now. Prior to these periods I usually scribble a lot. I gather stuff together. Then, I'll get a title or an idea that ties things together, and when I get to that situation, what I need to do is write.

REID: Is that how your first two books came together?

HARRIS: Yes, *Translation into Fiction* was largely written in spurts between Easter and December, 1982. *Fables* is a collection of work done over the years.

REID: You said that you read many African writers. Were there others who had an influence on your work?

HARRIS: I suspect that everything you read influences your work. I did a sort of double honours English degree at N.U.I. in Dublin. So I've read in some detail everyone of importance from the eighth century to the end of the nineteenth. And I've read writers like Claudel and Rimbaud, but I wouldn't want to claim them.

REID: But it wasn't till you went to Africa that you considered yourself a writer. Was it a political impulse that made you take your work seriously?

HARRIS: I think so. I seldom write only about myself. I'm always concerned with what's going on in the world.

REID: In some of your poems, there is a real abhorrence of that world. Isn't there sometimes an attempt to avoid that world? "The Experiment" opens: "to invite the presence of god I decide to drain/the mind." One way of getting out of the world is just to abolish the self.

HARRIS: I find the notion of god fascinating.

REID: Who is this god?

HARRIS: When I talk about god in my poems, it's usually the way I think people see him. Your typical primitive god justifying his owner's existence.

REID: He's often associated with pain and fear and silence, but sometimes he's a lover.

HARRIS: People see both those sides of god. I imagine that if there is a god, to come into his presence you need silence, you need to be still inside yourself. I'm talking here of a perfection (god) beyond our understanding.

REID: Isn't that a stillness you can achieve only in death?

HARRIS: You can't wait for death though, in order to connect with god, if he's out there. I'm ambivalent about the whole thing. It may just be one of our terrible misfortunes to discover that when you're dead you're really dead, which would be terribly disappointing.

REID: In one of your poems, as you're accommodating god, you refuse the name he gives you.

HARRIS: Yes, I won't be what somebody else calls me. I think the choice of my name is my own. And the poem is about the refusal to accommodate.

REID: In "Nude on a pale staircase" you speak of a woman choosing her grief the way she chose fruit in a market. Is that somehow parallel to choosing a god, or a name, or choosing a language that might give access to the gods? Or is it simply a recognition that people live in the world and any decision is going to lead to consequences both pleasant and unpleasant?

HARRIS: I think that people— poets for sure— have to choose a grief—

REID: But is it a conscious choice?

HARRIS: I think choose is a good word. I suspect that if people really examined their lives, they would find that somewhere along the line they made some choices— if only the decision not to choose.

REID: The desire for control informs your poems.

HARRIS: If anything in the poetry is really me, that's it.

REID: But there is that other impulse as well, isn't there? The one that distrusts control.

HARRIS: Perhaps social control. When you write, things always come into the work that you didn't realize— didn't anticipate or want. But as far as I consciously can, I want control over my life, my name, my poems.

REID: Why poetry, then? Why not political journalism or novels, something that would give you a bigger audience, and more potential power?

HARRIS: That's one of the areas where I don't think one does have a choice. Either there is a talent or there isn't. Power isn't part of the deal.

REID: A lot of your writing is done in a long almost breathless line. There's an urgency to it. It's earthy, and fleshy, and often political. But in one collection, you punctuate the longer poems with haiku. In one of the poems you state: "flesh is not haiku,"— I'm curious about the way you're using haiku here, and why you were drawn to it in the first place. It does set up an interesting tension with the other poems.

HARRIS: I find it interesting that you see the work as "fleshy." Sensual, perhaps. Haiku seems to me the most ordered, the most delicate, the most elegant of the literary forms. For most of us, life isn't elegant. Many of my poems freeze people in a moment immaculate in its horror. Actually, I distrust all that beauty. In Japan they probably lived dreadful lives and read beautiful poetry.

REID: A lot of different forms appear and disappear in your work. There are blocks of prose alternating with haiku, columns of verse going down either side of a page, short lyrics, long sequences. Are you hunting for a line that will accommodate what you want to say?

HARRIS: To some extent. But often the alterations occur because there are different ways of approaching things, there are at least two sides to everything. For instance, the poem I wrote about the guy kicking the baby to death. It could have been written from the mother's point of view. But I thought it would be interesting to write it from the male's. It must be incredible to wake up in the morning and realize what you've done. And you can't go out and kill yourself, so you have to rationalize it somehow. We aren't savages and we aren't angels; we're stuck with being human.

REID: Don't most people come to some form of accommodation with the extremes inside them?

HARRIS: I don't see why they should.

REID: If they don't, maybe they will go out and kill themselves.

HARRIS: I think that's one of the problems. We sit back and say, oh, well, that's the way things have to be, other people have suffered worse than you, nothing ever changes, and so nothing ever does. I think my poetry is a witness. I testify to the way things are for some people. For some without voice.

Signalling the Future

Michael Harris interviewed by Sonja A. Skarstedt

Michael Harris— poet, critic and professor— has also been the editor for the Signal Editions Poetry Series since its inception in 1981. Although Signal is an imprint of Montreal's Véhicule Press, Harris is free to edit Signal as he chooses while publisher Simon Dardick tends to the demands of Véhicule. Signal titles have included such diverse voices as Erin Mouré, Robert Allen, Don Coles, Ann Diamond, Bill Furey, Susan Glickman, Robert McGee, Robert Melançon and David Solway.

Michael Harris teaches literature at Montreal's Dawson College. His poetry publications include *Sparks* (1976), *Grace* (1978), *In Transit* (1985), *Miss Emily et la Mort* (1984), a selection of his poems translated by Jacques Marchand, and *The Muse and the Caterpillar* (1991).

SONJA A. SKARSTEDT: Whatever inspired you to become the editor of a poetry series?

MICHAEL HARRIS: Like everything else I've done I sort of fell into it— backwards. I've been editing for fifteen years now, I guess. My first official published book came out with New Delta, with Michael Gnarowski and Glen Seibrasse editing it, and I felt that there were people of my vintage who also deserved to be published. I somehow ingratiated myself with those two fellows and ended up being an editor for New Delta in the 1970s. There was some altruism involved— because I wanted to publish several people who I thought should be seen in print...

SKARSTEDT: Was there no other press that would have been willing to take on the younger poets at that time?

HARRIS: Not in Montreal.

SKARSTEDT: How would you describe the literary atmosphere in

Montreal in the '70s? Was Montreal really overshadowed by Toronto, as some might argue?

HARRIS: It was *very* overshadowed by Toronto in the sense that all of the big presses were there. In particular Oxford, McClelland & Stewart, Macmillan, Coach House... the list is very long and there was, apart from New Delta, nothing else really going on in Montreal.

SKARSTEDT: And you were experiencing the pangs of responsibility?

HARRIS: Yes, I guess I was very much interested in having a "scene," having a place for people to be able to publish— and that was associated with Vhicule Art Gallery readings. Our feeling back then was that universities had very staid series of writers, not that they were uninteresting, but a lot of the poets were American or from elsewhere and there seemed no official venue for Montreal poets to read, to garner their share of a reading audience. So at about the same time I was working for New Delta, I put on a reading series for Vhicule which over the years took off with other impresarios. The curious thing was that I found I could organize about a year and a half or so of reading once a month. But then I ran out of what I felt were interesting poets. What happened afterwards was that Vhicule bit by bit fell into a sort of demise.

SKARSTEDT: Demise?

HARRIS: Well, from my perspective there were too many uninteresting poets— and the audience diminished. In the first year we generally had about, oh, a hundred people for every reading. It was most successful, a great deal of fun. Eventually, however, it came down to everybody wanting to read and having all their friends read. The audiences diminished and people like Ralph Gustafson would come and a dozen people would show up to listen. It was a very peculiar way to end a reading series. Anyhow, I was well out of it by that time.

SKARSTEDT: In a way, then, Signal stemmed from this reading series?

HARRIS: It was associated with Vhicule Press itself, in the form of Simon Dardick, who published small broadsides bit by bit and then edged into smaller books and finally developed into a press. Signal started in 1981. I wasn't involved in Vhicule at all before that point. I had worked with New Delta for three or four years, between about 1975 and 1978. My feeling was that we needed a solid, substantial press in town and Simon Dardick had built up Vhicule Press itself into a reasonable small-sized publishing enterprise with some room at that point to do quality poetry titles and so I offered my services to him.

SKARSTEDT: As for the name Signal?

HARRIS: We tried to think of a name which would work well in French and English because we had intended to do some translations.

SKARSTEDT: Off to a good start, then...

HARRIS: It was perfect for me because I didn't want to be engaged in the business of actually producing the books. I selected the titles, edited them, and Simon produced the books.

SKARSTEDT: Writing, publishing, teaching— how do you manage it all?

HARRIS: Well, it's a little bit like pushing a shopping cart full of various sorts of squabbling animals, but... teaching gives me a lot of time during the summers and every now and then I get a grant to take time off and pursue my own work. The editing in fact doesn't take that much time. It's just a matter of doing a lot of reading. Except when I do the editing itself which generally takes three or four days at a stretch. I mean I work over a manuscript with whatever poet... It's a joy, something I like doing enormously.

SKARSTEDT: Even more than the act of writing poetry?

HARRIS: Well, almost! It's a very satisfying occupation. Generally I invite the poet to stay at my house for three or four days and we spend a lot of time together. We work over everything, every word, every line. I do "hands on" editing.

SKARSTEDT: Unusual.

HARRIS: It's not typical. It's inexcusably arrogant on my part, I suppose. But it comes from twenty years of teaching writing classes and poetry. It's a habit I've gotten into: even with the best poets I'll read a poem and mentally readjust what I don't like.

SKARSTEDT: Have you encountered any conflicts in this area?

HARRIS: There are a very few poets whose work I don't in fact make a lot of suggestions for— David Solway and Don Coles, for example, whose manuscripts tend to be very clean when they get to me. That is to say, I try to poke at them just pro forma but generally they maintain their lines, so...

SKARSTEDT: Do you have any "favourite" Signal poet?

HARRIS: No. There's something in each person's work that initially catches my eye and that I feel disposed to, to publish. Essentially, if I read a couple of hundred manuscripts a year and I can choose two or three, whatever manuscript I choose has to have a spark, some real life to it, something indistinguishable from any others that I've read.

SKARSTEDT: A couple of Signal editions have gone into second printings...

HARRIS: Ann·Diamond's *A Nun's Diary*, Susan Glickman's *Complicity*, the translation I did of Marie-Claire Blais have all gone into second printings. The books have done well, generally. As for reviews, well, my feeling always was at the onset that all I had to do was... survive. I just had to prevail. I think we're getting there. Five of our poets are Governor-General's Award winners. That's twenty-five percent of our list! I initially thought that if I could do it for twenty years then the press would establish itself well.

SKARSTEDT: A rather realistic vision...

HARRIS: Several things contributed to this. One is that the poets who are serviced by the major presses at this point have brought to bear a sort of top-heavy commitment for the editors who might in other circumstances wish to publish interesting new poets, but they have to service the old guard who continue to put out books. That is to say, McClelland & Stewart and Oxford, among others, are still producing their stable of 1960s and early 1970s poets and what happens is that I actually get manuscripts from McClelland & Stewart that they can't deal with.

SKARSTEDT: Neglected writers?

HARRIS: It's not so much neglected as McClelland & Stewart has a backlog of very well-established Canadian poets whose next books, or whose selected or collected poems they have to service; and they can only do four or five, maybe six books a year. So it means that the poets of the next generation tend to look for the small to medium-sized presses across the country and Signal has become one of those. We are not now a "local press," in the sense that I have books this year from poets in Vancouver, Calgary, Toronto... many of whom come from elsewhere— Brazil, Baltimore, Texas, Boston...

SKARSTEDT: An international perspective!

HARRIS: Yes, although they all happen to be Canadians. The intention— at least, *my* intention was never to be particularly a local press, although that's the way we started. My initial impulse, as with New Delta, was to provide local people with a press they could use. At this point, though, it's expanded and I would very much like to do more international work, translations... American poets, British poets, Australian poets. But you know we run into, as every press in Canada does, money problems because Canada Council prefers to fund national enterprise, which I understand.

SKARSTEDT: Yet you continue to forge ahead.

HARRIS: Well, I'd like to have an international series by the turn of the century.

SKARSTEDT: You were talking about translations...

HARRIS: I can't consider myself a translator. The reason I translated Marie-Claire Blais' work was that I— as a student at McGill— much enjoyed her novel, *A Season in the Life of Emmanuel*. So much so that I felt, when the opportunity came to translate her work, I thought I should pay her back for the pleasure I'd received from her novel. So it was not so much to "do translation" as to honour some writing I enjoyed. Or a writer whose work I enjoyed.

SKARSTEDT: How did you find the task of translating poetry?

HARRIS: It was the hardest job I think I've ever undertaken. It took a year and a half and a great deal of work. Whether it's successful or not I have no idea. Translation is a very slippery fish.

SKARSTEDT: Do you think you'll undertake another translation project in future?

HARRIS: Possibly. As I say, I tend to stumble into things.

SKARSTEDT: Can you elaborate?

HARRIS: I tend to be working most of the time, so if something comes up... For example, I wrote a series of poems about Emily Dickinson and a playwright by the name of Gary McKeehan phoned me up and said that he'd written a play incorporating a lot of that work, would I be interested in coming to see the read-through of it? And what's happened is that I sort of stumbled into theatre! And I'm about to write a play, probably this year, which I never particularly intended to do.

SKARSTEDT: How does an "anglo" press survive in La Belle Province? Any difficulties?

HARRIS: No, not at all. I find it a haven. I'm not nationalistically inclined in any sense. My reading tends to indicate that this is the case. I have no sense of loyalty, for example, toward Canadian authors particularly. I tend to read very widely. And I'm not entirely sure that nationalism's a very healthy thing, historically speaking. I haven't found the climate difficult in Quebec. There are prices to pay for being in a socialistic financial web, but there is also a certain anonymity that I treasure here, because in fact we're in a minority in the province and disassociated from the rest of Canada in a spiritual way, I think. Even if I travel abroad I'm not so much a Canadian as I am from Montreal. But that's my own spiritual predilection or political predilection. I'm happy in Montreal, partly because of the cosmopolitan nature of the city. I enjoy being absorbed into Greek areas or Portuguese areas or franco-phone areas— and anglophone areas! But it's necessary for me to be able to culture-hop in the same way that I book-hop.

SKARSTEDT: Is this culture-hopping reflected in the Signal series?

HARRIS: Well, I find that I've been attracted to the work of exiled Americans... Carla Hartsfield, from Texas, Arthur Clark, from Balti-more, for example, are in the recent groups of people I've published. And it's not so much that they're from Calgary or Texas... I simply like their work, I like their voice— acknowledging that the voices are in some way culturally oriented. It really is whatever spark dazzles me. I've been reading, for example, a great deal of the work of Yehuda Amichai, recently. Sharon Olds, from New York. I like them simply because their notes are glittering.

SKARSTEDT: A nationalistic sensibility *would* tend to narrow one's editorial scope, then...

HARRIS: I've noticed in Scotland, for example, which is a country spiritually and politically distinct from England, that sometimes the magazines give in to a kind of Scottish nationalism which doesn't necessarily make for the best verse or the best editing decisions. My feeling is that Canada is not unlike Scotland in that sense. We're an adjunct, we're an ancillary cultural pawn to the great wealth of American literature and so there's a defensive sensibility that I see and I find it's a dead end. I mean, if there were such a thing as "free trade" in ideas, I don't think CanLit is ready to make the leap. We're much, much too provincial in our cultural sensibilities.

SKARSTEDT: Do you find an international perspective is reflected in Montreal's general cultural climate?

HARRIS: What we seem to have ended up with in Montreal, are not just québécois film festivals, but international, *big* international film festivals, international jazz festivals... last year's P.E.N. International writer's meeting and so on. We're getting exposed to a lot of the work of the rest of the world. As I say, in the early '70s, my impulse was to start a reading series which didn't cater particularly to what the established CanLit departments of the various universities were doing, which was to have almost exclusively Canadian poets or poets from the States whose influence had been exerted on those particular Canadian poets. I think of the Tish group or the Black Mountain poets or New York poets or whatnot— and I didn't know what to do about that scene— but *any*thing other than that was what I wanted to do. I just felt that we were missing the boat somehow, that if our impulse was exclusively nationally oriented— and this has nothing to do with being in French Canada— then we were doomed to provincialism. I saw that there was extraordinary work available internationally and what was coming out of Toronto, specifically, then, was of very little interest.

SKARSTEDT: A bit of a rebellious spirit...

HARRIS: I don't think of myself as a rebel, in that sense. I think of myself as very conservative in the sense that my impulse is to conserve what I feel is worthwhile, rather than wave some particular flag under the nose of the dominant bull, just in order to have something happen.

SKARSTEDT: What kind of poetry is Signal seeking? The series seems to steer clear of obvious experimentation, more toward high-craftedness.

HARRIS: My feeling is that all poets, in their apprenticeships, do and should experiment with form, all sorts of form. And all sorts of literary ideologies. Principally because it seems to be essential as with any other discipline, engineering cars or choreographing a dance, that the mode which finally suits any poet the best had to be mined from all possible sources. I think it's important to mimic, to plagiarize, to steal ideas, but as with any dancer I suppose, it's one's own body one has to work with, finally. And the best poets should be able to make use of all the forms available, I mean, the entire canon, the anthology, the tradition, global literature.

SKARSTEDT: Discipline—

HARRIS: I have always liked the notion that the Irish Scops used to have to undergo a fourteen-year apprenticeship. That was a nice idea! Nowadays the poet undergoes a very personal apprenticeship in the sense that I think the more widely one reads the more one sees that there are valuable energies and styles available. Everywhere. So, an eclectic education is probably the most useful to any artist.

SKARSTEDT: What of the educational system? Is there too much focus on dissection and dry interpretation, not enough attention paid to the *pleasure* one can receive from reading poetry?

HARRIS: It seems to me the apprentice poet has to learn to "dissect," but it seems to me also that the *love* of poetry is what should be taught. I'm not sure that, apart from having an enlightened and joyous teacher, whose lessons are... magnetic, seductive— that the young poet can get any better an education than to submit to the widest reading possible.

SKARSTEDT: Can we blame— or partly blame— the media for inducing a lazy attitude toward poetry, and books in general?

HARRIS: Well, I'm not sure that everyone can be taught to think metaphorically, but my understanding is that sales of single volumes of poetry have never been better.

SKARSTEDT: Really!

HARRIS: In the same sense that more people than ever seem to have a bug in their body about watching bodies dance, and pay twenty dollars to go see the ballet... But— I'm not suggesting that there aren't charismatic superstars who pave the way for literature in some way to be popular. I think there are certain sensibilities inherent in certain people that demand that they read poetry. It's probably chemical.

SKARSTEDT: Why publish poetry in such a materialistic society where so few enjoy even the simple act of thinking?

HARRIS: That's the same question one asks about whether one is a poet or an artist of any sort. The answer to that is if you have to ask the question, then you're not one. I'm not suggesting it's something people are born to do. It's just that if there is any alternative to writing, I would suggest people take it. But if there is no alternative then it's a matter of learning how to do it as well as one can. As with anything else, as with dancers or runners, it's not a matter of people conceiving of themselves as, let's say, track stars. Basically, people call you a track star when you've won the hundred metre dash. On the other hand, I don't think you can become a track star unless you wake up at eight years old and decide that that's what you want to be!

SKARSTEDT: Is it difficult to find *good* writers?

HARRIS: Well the answer to that is that there are very few fine writers anywhere. And Canada's a small country, Montreal's a relatively small town, so... on the one hand there may be a number of writers who are of some interest but in twenty years' time, as in the yellowing anthologies one thumbs through, how many of those voices are still useful? Very few. I mean, you look at the anthologies of the turn of the century or the '40s or '50s, there are one or two voices whose work still seems fresh and useful. There's also a kind of contemporary revisionism— if I make a mild oxymoron there— a sort of instant nostalgia for belonging to the CanLit coterie. The League of Poets, for example, has— what is it— three hundred members now? That's an extraordinary number of poets for a country our size! Seems everybody'd like to belong.

SKARSTEDT: The future— will Signal maintain its position of influence?

HARRIS: Oh, I have no doubt about that. I think it has less to do with me as an editor than with the fact that I can act as a neutral barometer for the three or four voices a year that seem appealing or seem to have potential. The best I can do is be the kick-starter, to see that the— forgive this!— vehicle works! And I think the younger, interesting poets are in fact one by one being drawn to Signal because— at least this is how I hope it will work— because they see that other interesting voices are being serviced by a particular press and it's very difficult for a younger person to get a book out with M&S or the other established presses.

SKARSTEDT: Hope?

HARRIS: Well, I seem to be getting more and better manuscripts every year.

SKARSTEDT: From the younger poets?

HARRIS: It's not just that. I get manuscripts from poets of my vintage, I mean, in their forties or fifties who are ready for a selected poems or who haven't been able to get a toe-hold in the larger Toronto presses.

SKARSTEDT: Do you have much of a connection with Simon Dardick and Vhicule?

HARRIS: Simon has his own series of books— literary criticism, social and women's issues... he gives me an absolutely free hand to edit my own series under the Signal imprint. It's a gift. I'm blessed. The editors at McClelland & Stewart, for example, have instructions to take care of the stable of poets that they've already published and my own feeling is that if a so-called "established poet" has a book out through Signal, I wouldn't necessarily take the next book that he or she submits unless it's of a quality that makes it worth our mutual whiles. There's so much work that is potentially of interest that I can't afford not to be extremely choosey.

SKARSTEDT: All in all, do you find editing a rewarding experience?

HARRIS: The real reward that I get from the press— there's no money in it, of course— is to continue to publish first-class work. And the poets like David Solway, Don Coles, Susan Glickman and Ann Diamond, for example... year by year are making their mark, at least nationally, in some cases internationally. I admit to some pride, which is a great reward.

SKARSTEDT: You feel then, that there has been a definite evolution since the imprint began?

HARRIS: I may delude myself by thinking that Signal is becoming an "established" press, but— after so many years I think I can get away with that assessment! What it means is that it's not so much a struggle at this point: it's just the discipline of continuing the work. The press itself, I mean the publishing end of it, is very well set up, the distribution is good, everybody's got the address for their manuscripts, so there's nothing for me to do really but every couple of weeks go to Simon's place and pick up the new manuscripts.

SKARSTEDT: Any celebrations planned for Signal's anniversary?

HARRIS: We're going to have celebrations of some sort, both in Montreal and in Toronto, because at this point our base in fact is as much in Toronto as it is here. Which is something I'd also never conceived of— ten years ago. This fall we're doing a series of readings in Toronto in October. As we publish more Toronto people we get a broader base of Signal authors there.

SKARSTEDT: Any last words on the kind of poets Signal is seeking?

HARRIS: I have always been attracted to the writing of so-called "outsiders." Which is not to say "experimentalists" or whatever, although those are partly included— but people whose voices tend to be somewhat solitary or unique. I have great difficulty working with "schools"— the school-oriented poets... that is to say "language" or "sound" or "concrete" poets or whatever kind of group poets. Because I find that the true interesting sensibilities come from people who have a unique vision of things and so they're— I mean, my feeling is that there isn't any particular "voice" that Signal has— there are a range of poetries written by people who have something unique to say. Or a unique way of saying it. And that is what has always interested me about editing: finding those particular voices of people who have worked something out— one thing, or one way of looking at things. A fresh and insightful voice.

Every One of Us Was There

Roy Kiyooka interviewed by Roy Miki

Roy Kenzie Kiyooka was born on January 18, 1926, in Moose Jaw, Saskatchewan, but his earliest retrieved memories of the restless childhood "i" forming belong to the sidestreets and lanes of his neighbourhood in east Calgary during the 1930s. Kiyooka is nisei, the second generation, Canadian-born progeny of the issei, the first generation, immigrant parents. He was the third of six children born to Harry Shigekiyo and Mary Kiyoshi Kiyooka, who ran a vegetable stand in a multi-ethnic city market. The young Roy quickly developed resources to fend for himself in the anglophone milieu of the majority, his native tongue sealed in the confines of the familial and internalized by the racism dominant in his society. The movement between those two "worlds" may have eventually transformed into a workable dialectic— given an uninterrupted developmental process— but one event would intervene to radically transform the shape of Kiyooka's life: the mass uprooting of Japanese Canadians in 1942.

The Kiyooka family, living in Calgary, were not among the 23,000 Japanese Canadians— 95% of the whole Japanese Canadian population in Canada— expelled from the "protected area" 100 miles from the west coast. The political wave of racism, however, reached beyond BC and affected Japanese Canadians all across Canada. Even those living far from the coast were branded "enemy alien" and, overnight, found themselves the target of bigots who took advantage of the wartime crisis to press for the removal of Japanese Canadians from BC and who passed the Orders in Council to prevent them from moving back.

Roy Kiyooka was the author of several books, including *Kyoto Airs*, *Pear Tree Pomes*, and *Pacific Windows*, edited by Roy Miki and published posthumously.

ROY MIKI: To begin with, I was wondering whether in your mind there was any such thing as "the Japanese Canadian writer"? I'm curious about the kind of perspective that you, as a writer, bring to the question.

ROY KIYOOKA: Okay, it'll take me a bit to warm up to this, because I haven't really dwelt on the matter at all, but I know that through my own experience of writing, such as it is, that— well, for several reasons— that my first language was in fact Japanese and that I learned English, not in the home so much as on the street, previous to going to school (grade one). What I didn't get as a child, which I see, having had children myself and kids around me— that one of the ways in which a child grasps the fundamentals of the language, particularly the inclination to move language toward story, they learn by the time they are three or four years of age, if they have been read to— I didn't get read to. So two things happened: one, I didn't get that element of story within the language, and two, I didn't get any of the folkloric element that gets passed that way, the fairy tales and the children's stories, and things like that. There's no one to blame for this. This was simply the circumstances of being a Japanese Canadian, and the fact that neither my mother nor my father were— well, my father spoke very good English and he could write well, too, but my mother is not, even at this moment in time, very articulate, and can barely read. In terms of the English language, you could say that she is essentially illiterate, after sixty years in this country. And for myself— given the fact I was not given that as a condition of acquiring English, I feel in some ways, or have felt, extraordinarily handicapped. That was brought home to me yesterday in our talk with Robert Duncan, who of course had such an extraordinary access to the world of his childhood, the fantasies and the dreams and the stories, because he was nurtured on those things, and I was not. I was given the rudiments of Japanese folkloric tales orally through what my mother would tell me, you know, telling me stories. It was not a *reading to*, and it was in Japanese, not English.

MIKI: So what then happens later on?

KIYOOKA: So what happens later on is that one has, in some ways, to work to claim that ground that they would have had almost naturally as a child. That's what I have had to do. And that ground includes some very fundamental sense of articulation, which would be nothing more than notions of grammar and things like that. Well, the truth of the matter is that I have never grasped the fundamentals of English in terms of those structures, even to this day. So that for me, whatever articulateness I have come to, I have come to through reading and listening to people. My inclination is to be articulate out of that context with only an intuitive grasp of what the structure of the language is.

MIKI: I think you mentioned that you had Japanese as your primary language, but now, when you think or when you write, you naturally use English.

KIYOOKA: Oh, yes, there is no question about that, because like a number of kids who grew up on the prairies of my generation, we tended to be isolated, very small pockets of Japanese. The upshot of that was, there was not the same compulsion on the part of our parents, in some sense, to "hang on to." Now this may be going against what the sociologists would say, but my father and mother were left in the situation where the only terms of their survival were to acquire the basic articulateness by which they could survive in the white world, and so the insistence on their part for their children was that way. Of course, the desire that we were all to be educated was very primary. They didn't succeed very well because they were so poor. But they wanted that for their kids, and the kids of course went out and did it for themselves.

MIKI: So then immediately acquiring English assumes a very large part in your life.

KIYOOKA: Oh, yeah, to me it had to do with surviving— *survival*. At some level I needed to be able to come to an articulateness by which I could stand in this world of literate people, and hold my own. I had that as an actual drive.

MIKI: But then there's a disjuncture that occurs between the fact that, in some way, Japanese remained your primary language, and on the other side was this language that was controlled by that larger world "out there." And so you get a very particular relationship to language, say, a Canadian kid growing up speaking English all the time, never worrying about the language, doesn't have.

KIYOOKA: Oh, yes, I think my own sense of myself, apropos Canada and the whole thrust toward bilingualism, is that I belong to that class of Canadians that is just naturally bilingual. By that I don't mean necessarily an adeptness in both languages, but that one's sensibility is grounded in two languages. That's what I really mean. I have only to meet a Japanese and my mouth opens— I never speak English, Japanese just comes out of my mouth. I can only be attuned to that person in terms of the ground of my sensibility that is Japanese, and I can recognize in that person qualities that through speech I can address. I wouldn't have that, except for these peculiar circumstances.

MIKI: Did you ever write poems, or attempt to, seriously in Japanese?

KIYOOKA: No, oh, no, no, because my Japanese is rudimentary, finally. Again this is case history, but I grew up in Calgary, the Japanese community was very small, we didn't really have much to do with each other except at *Shogatsu*, New Year's. But I was a street kid essentially, and by the time I was eight or nine I could speak as well as any white kid in the neighborhood... the Japanese thing was really aborted because there seemed at that time in my life, to my parents, literally no cause to have any truck with the Japanese culture because it was such a remove.

MIKI: You were about eight or nine?

KIYOOKA: About then— I was moving just simply in the neighbour-hood, my world, and it was distinctly a kind of immigrant ghetto, East Calgary in the '30s, so that everybody was aware of other races in terms of stereotypes. I mean, I grew up and went to a school full of all kinds of different races, but I learned through each and every one of them what their stereotypes of the others were.

MIKI: You probably could see that so quickly.

KIYOOKA: Oh, yeah, sure I could, but I had no really stereotypical image of Japanese, see, because it was as actual as my immediate family, but otherwise essentially the domain— was an aspect of my own imagination, because it was "way over there."

MIKI: And yet somehow the English language which you would later write in was "out there" too?

KIYOOKA: Sure.

MIKI: When, then, did you become interested in the whole possibility of writing?

KIYOOKA: Well, I think that occurred to me, in my late twenties, as something I might myself do, not previous to that. But the actual movement toward literacy began in my teens, because I didn't go to school beyond grade nine. My ninth grade and the bombing of Pearl Harbor are precisely coincidental, and the one terminated the other. From that point on, I was involved in self-education, which meant reading a great deal, and in the beginning having no leadership or directions in terms of reading, but simply moving from book to book on fancy or curiosity or even chance.

MIKI: Were there any Japanese Canadian or Japanese American writers at that time that you read?

KIYOOKA: No, I had no sense of it at all. That was much later. I didn't even become curious about the possibility that there were any number of North American Japanese who may be writers or artists or anything like that. That didn't seem important to me. I never even entertained the thought until I was well into my twenties.

MIKI: Do you think this was a common condition among Japanese Canadians then, that very few would consider becoming writers?

KIYOOKA: Oh, yeah, though this is a generalization that has some credibility in terms of what's happened, there aren't too many people of my generation whose parents encouraged them to go into anything esoteric, simply because the nitty-grits of life proposed that they had to, in some way, succeed in comprehensible ways, you know, like money talks, or reputation or respectability. My whole generation after the war— the drift was almost completely towards the "professional profes-sions," if you will, the engineers and the doctors and the dentists. I mean, those of my generation who got educated, all went that way, really, all of them.

MIKI: When you started writing, did you think of yourself as "Japanese Canadian"?

KIYOOKA: No, that never entered into the writing. The only thing that seemed to be important— and it's still a touchstone for me— was that it be grounded in the actual experience of one's life, that you'd bring the possibilities of language to some occasion in your life. I still work from that kind of nexus, so that my poetry does not seem to ever get fanciful in terms of simply being *about* the domains of the imagination. I mean, it can enter into that, but for me writing is an instrument of gaining my own self-awareness, that's what it is. It's to save oneself from confusion and obfuscation and all those kinds of things simply by sitting down and trying to sort it out. And I still have that attitude, essentially.

MIKI: That's the question I was going to ask you, and then I'm going to see if I can tie it back around to what you began talking about. In your work you seem to be very conscious of the way language acts as a medium of human experience.

KIYOOKA: Yes, yes, I learned that— one of the essential places where I've learned that is in the activity of teaching. Teaching has— well, teaching is what Plato was about. The terms of his own effectiveness, it seemed to me, had to do with sounding very deep experiences in the language. And those occasions in and through the activity of teaching that have enabled me to do that have been very important instances of finding my own worth in the language, as it were.

MIKI: That kind of articulation you would see very much as a communal activity. I'm thinking of your *transcanada letters*, the writing there.

KIYOOKA: Oh, yes, for me the business of all the arts is a serious one. Insofar as one assumes that kind of responsibility, you have to come to articulateness for the sake of the inarticulate among the world that you live in. And that goes for a lot of the Japanese who, in terms of being able to shape in some way how they feel here in this country, they're tongue-tied, they're really tongue-tied. And where they're not tongue-tied, they're afraid to speak their minds because they've already undergone an adequate humility to— I don't know, make them wary that way.

MIKI: Do you think that some of them are caught in that early space you talked about where they see Japanese and English as very separate, so that perception freezes—

KIYOOKA: Oh, yes.

MIKI: So then the English language becomes very terrifying?

KIYOOKA: Oh, sure.

MIKI: Was that feeling tied to your beginnings as a writer?

KIYOOKA: I think I was prompted to want to write at some point in my life simply because in and through my own reading— not only that, but how my reading and what was occurring as actual events in my life in the world around me was a kind of a dialectic that continuously interfaced with each other. And it seemed to me to propose: *that* is something really worth doing. Some such thought like that is what prompted me really to do it. But it had also to do with learning. I'm not a systematic learner. I'm an intuitive learner. What that means is that I have to keep coming back, or stay with something, until something goes "ding" up here, and then I can move on. But there was no way I could analytically grasp what it was because it had to undergo some very complex kind of metamorphoses and— well, anyhow, I feel, for myself, I long ago recognized that I was given a job to do and that job had to do with being, for my own immediate family in the first instance, a kind of a voice, and a cultural voice in a collective sense. I know that that's true because the different responses I've had from my brothers and sisters and my parents have always told me that. And so I'm only doing, in that sense, what is absolutely inevitable. I haven't chosen to do this. I've literally been chosen to do it.

MIKI: That's quite fascinating.

KIYOOKA: Oh, I really do believe this, and concomitantly, it makes me a loner. It's as though you found yourself, despite yourself, having to do everything the most difficult way imaginable because you had to explore the whole terrain before you got a purchase on it.

MIKI: Would that be a good way of stating the beginnings of a Japanese Canadian writer?

KIYOOKA: Oh, yes, I would say so, sure— I really think so, unless you're in some ways more simple. I'm thinking of that lovely woman who wrote a book of her childhood experiences in the camps with her own paintings—

MIKI: *A Child in Prison Camp* by Takashima—

KIYOOKA: Yes, that's a rare little book. It's quite pure how she was able to retrieve a moment in time thirty years previously. The terms of her literateness are different from mine because I have invested much more of my actual life in the world, in the "white-Anglo-Saxon-English-speaking" world. The whole matrix of my life is bound up with that, and I want to be able to account for that, as I am in it. That would be one of the fundamental differences between her and me. She's the kind of person who will likely be a one-book writer. There is just that one exquisite moment in her life that she's been able to finger, and whether she will ever be able to have a touchstone that will enable her to go on, I don't know. There are lots of people like that.

MIKI: Not to diverge too much, but I'm fascinated by that book. There's that one section in the book when the young Buddhist who's in the camp used to chant in the morning. And the RCMP come one day and remove him. In the story he just sort of disappears, and there's this kind of dark hole. And no account is made, you get the feeling that she is not going to account for that darker disappearance within her own story which is moving toward a different completion. I thought that was one moment where there was a possibility for something totally other than what was on the surface of the story to break in.

KIYOOKA: I may be wrong, but my sense of it, and I don't mean this in a pejorative sense, is that she is a simple person, and though she touched something there, the mystery that she fingered was something she moved over and away from because the actual intimations of that mystery were not given to her, as it were.

MIKI: Could you reconstruct in your mind your own events as a writer that led up to your first publication, *Kyoto Airs*?

KIYOOKA: Yes, that was 1963, I was thirty-seven years of age. But I had actually been writing since— well, the first bit of serious writing I did was about my Mexico experience in 1956. And I still have the manuscript of that. It was in the form of a kind of "travel-log-lecture," because when I came back to teach at the University of Regina, I wanted to gather that experience together to present it to my kids. So I worked it all out, but I didn't think of myself as a writer, in the sense of somebody who published. Oh, no, I felt deeply inside of myself too awkward to be able to claim that. And this was literally true up until *Kyoto Airs*, which finally got done with a great deal of trepidation on my part. Despite the brevity of the poems, there were thousands of hours of work in those poems, you know, because it wasn't as though the poem was just given in that lovely sense of inspiration or anything like that. To me it was an act of retrieval in terms of the detritus of my language, just the shit of it. I had to go over and over and over again... That was a lovely time for me, 1963, fifteen years ago, thirty-seven years of age, but I went through that whole thing as just the most eager-beaver kind of undergraduate, oh, sure...

MIKI: I'd like to leap ahead before this interview comes to an end, and ask you about a couple of recent events in your life, a reading in Toronto and the Order of Canada award. What was the occasion of the reading?

KIYOOKA: Maya Koizumi and a group of others have formed the Toronto equivalent in some ways of Tonari Gumi [Japanese Community Volunteers Association] except that Toronto being the kind of city it is, and the Japanese community so sprawling, the percentage of old people to come there is small. It's become a kind of gathering place for the younger people. When I was in Toronto for the OC [Order of Canada] I told Maya I'd like to do something to help her place along, and she thought that a reading would be a great idea. I went there and there were about fifteen people, mostly sansei. There were a few nisei, I think. I told them that this was the first time, insofar as I could remember, addressing a group of Japanese larger than one or two, and that *that* was, in itself, quite novel for me, and well, I read poems and sort of ad-libbed as I went along, trying to sound something out of my own life that might be useful to them. That's what I was doing. But they were rather forlorn, I felt they were forlorn in the sense that most of them, if not deeply alienated, were in some sense alienated from themselves. It seemed to me that was largely because they were completely swallowed holus-bolus in that Toronto culture. And to be anything other than a white Anglo-Saxon, you know, was not to be much, like in terms of voice, or anything like that. And I think they were afflicted by that, in some ways, that's what I mean.

MIKI: Did you have a chance to talk with any of them?

KIYOOKA: Oh, yes, terrific, they were fine. Oh, no, despite what I just said, in the talking we had later, I realized they were fully aware of where they were at, but it was still a lonely place.

MIKI: But they at least had the advantage that you didn't have, which was to hear a Japanese Canadian writer.

KIYOOKA: Yes, David Suzuki had been there a week or so previously, so they're getting it...

MIKI: While you were in the east you received the Order of Canada.

KIYOOKA: Yes, I was on my way through Toronto to Ottawa to get it at that time.

MIKI: I thought maybe I could record some of your impressions of that occasion, which was quite different from the reading.

KIYOOKA: Oh, yes, sure, the two are the two sides of the coin, because the occasion of the reading at the Annex was given in the light of my going to Ottawa to receive the Order, and I even talked about it at the reading. I as much as said, as I told the Order of Canada committee when they wrote to me, that I had some basic skepticism about such honours but that I was fully prepared to accept it for the sake of my family. I felt I was accepting it for their sake, and not my own. I really did feel, even in and during that occasion, that I was there as some sort of representative, a mannequin in a tuxedo, if you will, on which the thing was to be pinned, and not very much for my own sake. And I felt my choice was political anyhow. It coincided with a number of things: one, the hundredth anniversary of the Japanese in this country; two, the hundredth anniversary of Tom Thomson's death, which mean a huge amount in Canadian art, both the same year. And my sort of straddling both those things— well, then meeting the other people who were also honoured, and the reception after, and I realized through and through that it was just an incredibly complex political gesture made through a host of people, and every one of us was there in some sense that way. Because the notion of the awards was that lovely idea of the Canadian mosaic, therefore the OC must represent, you know—

MIKI: So you're saying, in one sense, that you were invisible.

KIYOOKA: Sure, I was invisible, despite the fact that I went out of my way to make myself visible. See, part of the information we received was on protocol and attire and things like that. It was mandatory that we all wear black tuxedos, etc., etc. I had no intention of ever doing that. I had never had a tuxedo on my back in the first instance, and if I was going to do that, I wasn't going to wear a black one. I rented a green one, and I was the only one who wore anything but a black tuxedo. I wore a green tuxedo. It was really green, a beautiful green, but it was also spring.

MIKI: Did you give a speech?

KIYOOKA: No, none of us had to do that, because it was all happening the other way around, a guy standing up at a podium and reading out everybody's name and all their honours and then reading their citations.

MIKI: Were you honoured as a painter mostly?

KIYOOKA: And a teacher, too.

MIKI: And as a writer, too?

KIYOOKA: I don't remember if it was mentioned.

MIKI: And yet, juxtaposed against that, a reading in Toronto. You were there mostly as a writer.

KIYOOKA: And totally as a Japanese Canadian.

MIKI: So somehow those two poles of your childhood are still operative?

KIYOOKA: Oh, yes, oh, yes, oh, sure they are. Duncan was saying yesterday something interesting; he was speaking about those people who very early in their life had a fantasy of what they wanted to become, and that the entirety of their lives was, as it were, hooked to that fantasy. Their own realization moved in those terms. Others are bereft of such fantasies and their lives are therefore potentially more complex because they can be churning more, or they fly off in all sorts of directions. I've always thought myself to be of the former, that I'm living out some fantasy that I had when I was quite young about what I ought to be or do.

MIKI: So then, what about the subject— "the Japanese-Canadian writer"?

KIYOOKA: As a subject?

MIKI: Yes.

KIYOOKA: I don't think "the Japanese-Canadian writer" is important as a parsing of writers into groups— is Rudy Wiebe *the* eminent Slavic writer of the prairies? And so on and so forth.

MIKI: But there is, nevertheless, at least I can see, something more than simply personal in the way you grew up, and the way you distinguish between Japanese and English, and your emphasis on writing as articulation.

KIYOOKA: Yes, again going back to childhood, I think the condition of a child's life is the essential domain of the magical and that I am one of those kinds of people who have hung onto that all their lives, never quite lost that. And I have, in that sense, been truly fortunate, I mean, really lucky because— well, what can one say about it except that you are given that, your life has its orders, man, I'm given something to do. There's just no doubt about that at all in my mind, and I would be foolish to propose to do otherwise.

Perpetual Prayer

Gwendolyn MacEwen interviewed by Robert Sward

Poet and novelist Gwendolyn MacEwen was the author of several books of poetry, including *Armies of the Moon* and *The Shadow-maker*. Her works of fiction include *Julian the Magician* and *King of Egypt, King of Dreams*.

ROBERT SWARD: What do you understand by the word "spiritual"?

GWENDOLYN MACEWEN: It's a very simple word for me. As I understand it now, it refers to a perpetual and overwhelming reverence for life and a kind of heightened consciousness of all things going on around one at all times. It's a state of being continually conscious and therefore experiencing a heightened degree of beauty and of pain and of anguish and a sense of the miraculous. Most people only occasionally experience such things, but I feel that the mystic is experiencing them all the time. I would hate to think that poetry is written solely out of blinding visions because it would be dreadful poetry if it were not tempered with intelligence and a feeling for craft. But of course poetry without some kind of transcending vision is pretty dull poetry.

SWARD: I find I go back to that poem of yours "The Absolute Room" over and over again. "We came to a place which was the centre of ourselves"— that poem has a place in your book, *The T.E. Lawrence Poems*, and I wonder what the figure of Lawrence means to you?

MACEWEN: The figure of Lawrence always fascinated me. Lawrence himself was by no means a mystic. But he was fascinated with Arab mysticism, Semitic mysticism. Lawrence was drawn to the desert Arabs, these Bedouin, because they felt such great joy in renouncing the pleasures and treasures of the world. It was almost a sort of voluptuousness in not having anything, not owning anything. Their relationship to their god was a passionate one, intense and passionate, and Lawrence was constantly in awe of this. He could never achieve it himself. I am more of a mystic than Lawrence was. I feel closer to the kind of passionate fervour that the desert Semites felt towards the god in that vast nothingness, the feeling of identification with the Infinite, the One, the All, and the nothing, however one wants to put it. I think for Lawrence these were only concepts that fascinated him but didn't touch him.

SWARD: Do you yourself follow any regular devotional practices?

MACEWEN: No, not at all. I think life is a devotional practice in itself, living consciously day by day, being aware of the sheer wonder, the sheer mystery of all things at all times: that is in itself a perpetual prayer.

SWARD: After reading *The T.E. Lawrence Poems*, and the earlier travel book, *Mermaids and Ikons*, based on a summer spent in Greece, I identified very strongly with the power that the Mediterranean and the Middle East have had on you.

MACEWEN: Well, the Lawrence book had been on my mind for a long time, but I only wrote the poems last winter; they came to me very easily, very smoothly. I suppose I am drawn to Lawrence by the extraordinary step he took from a British world into a totally Arab one. He follows his "destiny," but it turned out to be a very ironic, negative destiny. Like him, I am fascinated by that part of the world. It was natural for me to assume his persona; the whole book is written in first person. It's a lot of fun taking on another voice; you can say things which are impossible otherwise. It's relatively easy for me to do because I've written fiction and drama where I use voices other than my own.

SWARD: Would you say there's an innate connection for you between prose and poetry?

MACEWEN: Yes, and for me there's an inter-relationship between all forms of writing; it's just a question of stance. One of the obvious differences between prose and poetry is that fiction takes so much longer, is really harder work, in terms of the ability to sustain ideas over a long period of time. The mind is involved in different processes. I find, though, that when one is known primarily for poetry, as I am, then one's prose becomes invariably known as poetic prose. People will say, "This is a poet's novel," whether or not it's particularly poetic. It is unfortunate because I don't regard myself as a poet only, but as a writer.

SWARD: When D.M. Thomas described that journey from poetry to prose, he said it felt like going through the eye of the needle, a painstaking expansion outward. There are obviously many ways of doing it.

MACEWEN: Yes, there are. Finally, it's difficult to say subjects work better in prose than in poetry, why, for instance, the TE Lawrence book came out as poetry. It might well have been a novel in the first person, but it wasn't. I don't know all the reasons why.

SWARD: Would it then have contained much more detail?

MACEWEN: Yes, I think we're close to the main point here. He provided so much detail himself, in *The Seven Pillars of Wisdom,* in his letters and so forth, that it would have been pointless to go over it again. I wanted something tighter than a story.

SWARD: Can we change direction and talk about poetry readings? Do you enjoy them?

MACEWEN: Yes, very much. I always have. I feel that poets have no right to give readings unless they can do it well. I've been to so many boring poetry readings— I think we all have— where you wish the poet would just go away. I think the best readers are those who thoroughly enjoy what they are doing, even to the extent of hamming it up a bit. I am always aware when I read that the people in the audience have come out to hear me, often through bad weather, and over some distance, and I therefore owe them something. Too many poets forget to look at their listeners, address them as people, let them laugh, allow them to relax. It's not such an intensely serious thing that no one can have fun. The reader must know something of how to present himself on a stage; otherwise he should get off it.

SWARD: I agree. Now and then one can at least offer an anecdote of some kind.

MACEWEN: Yes. The story of how one has come upon a title, for example.

SWARD: What would you say to a writer just starting out?

MACEWEN: Well, I always find this very difficult. I'm on their side totally, regardless of what they are writing, because I remember what it was like. I prefer not to get involved. I'm not happy in those situations, because what little I can say is not really going to make much difference to a person's future. It's a very heavy responsibility; and there's no final word on poetry, nothing that can be said that will tie everything up. After all this time, the only thing I'm sure of is that a poem is good when it makes me shiver, feel frightened, startled. I would tell a young writer to be bold always, to dare, to take risks.

SWARD: What sort of climate did you find when you began in the early '60s?

MACEWEN: Well, it seems there was a real poetry explosion then. Suddenly, people were talking about poetry; poets were reading and getting audiences out to hear them. It was all very exciting. Poets who have now published several books and become quite prominent were all around at that time. Contact Press was still going and, in fact their publication of my first book, *The Rising Fire* was, I think, one of their last books.

SWARD: How did you get yourself through the rejection slip phase?

MACEWEN: Oh, I went through years of that, but it never really bothered me. I can never understand writers who get upset about rejections. I just took it as a matter of course. I was in a very formative stage of my work and I knew it. I was probably overwriting, but it was also necessary to overwrite in order to learn. It seemed quite logical to me that if I sent out half-a-dozen poems maybe one would be accepted, maybe none.

SWARD: You've been writing a long time.

MACEWEN: I've been writing seriously since I was about eighteen and had some poems published in the *Canadian Forum* when I was younger. It was always natural for me. I realized that writing was what I could do and do well. That's why I didn't go on to university. Everyone thought that I would, that it would be an obvious step. But I didn't want to spend a lot of time having to learn what literature was all about. I simply wanted to make it myself, and I knew that it would take years of work before I'd get anywhere at all.

SWARD: Speaking of work, the kind you must sustain over long periods of time, we're back again to one of the big differences between prose and poetry.

MACEWEN: Oh, yes, the sheer effort of memory in prose is enormous— simply remembering from day to day what one has written the day before, whereas with poetry you can often see the whole poem at a glance.

SWARD: So, do you find yourself re-reading constantly?

MACEWEN: Well, I can usually hang on to a thread for about a hundred pages or so, but then I have to stop and track back, especially as I tend to do a lot of research. The Egyptian novel, for instance, *King of Egypt, King of Dreams*, took me five years to complete, but I loved every minute of it. Keeping track of all the names and details was a tremendous effort, though.

SWARD: It's total immersion, isn't it?

MACEWEN: Yes. I enjoy writing when there's an intellectual challenge in front of me all the time. I could write an awful lot more poetry than I do— you know, mood poetry, descriptive poetry. But I don't feel this challenges me enough intellectually. The Lawrence poems did, though, because I had to work with historical facts and philosophical paradoxes.

SWARD: Do you really feel poetry is limited that way? I find much of yours has a strong metaphysical root.

MACEWEN: Poetry is not limited at all. But I can't write only poetry. I spend hours a day as a writer, not only as a poet. I need to be involved in a novel or some larger work. At the moment, I'm doing a play.

SWARD: You use mythology extensively in your work but I never feel that you escape to it, or hide in it. It seems to me you rediscover it in your own world.

MACEWEN: Exactly. I'm aware of the mythic proportions of life itself. The mythic shape of events.

SWARD: It has been said by critics that the ecstasy you achieve in your poems is never without the sense of cost, even loss. I see that vividly in all your fire imagery.

MACEWEN: Yes, I accept both joy and suffering. From that acceptance comes, I think, a more enduring beauty.

SWARD: That accounts, too, doesn't it for the notion in *Shadow Maker* that one must absorb the darkness? But then, I think your phrase "the ruinous light" of Greece also includes annihilation.

MACEWEN: Exactly, light can be a disaster, especially in Greece. I like that phrase "disastrous light"; I must remember it. Greek light is almost painful in its clarity, whereas light to us is softer. In Greek tragedy the climax of everything took place at high noon. With us it would be at midnight.

SWARD: Many readers, and I'm one of them, have found a dreamlike quality in your work. You draw from the outside in, creating a wholeness. Maybe that's part of the poetic process, but it seems particularly smooth and natural in your work.

MACEWEN: For me, outer and inner reality are the same thing. My dreams are extraordinarily vivid. I assumed every one else's are. In an interview with a new magazine called *Dreamweaver* I described a kind of dreamlife and a dream world that I find to my surprise is much more intense than most people's. I thought everyone dreamt in colour with a cast of thousands. I have what feels like almost total recall of dreams. It's wonderful!

SWARD: I find that I really have to unplug myself from a number of activities; when I'm travelling, for instance, or holed up in a cottage somewhere working on a project, then the inner and outer lives really start to connect.

MACEWEN: Yes, that's interesting, because I do lead a very quiet and private life. I am not involved in the frantic pace of living that many others have to cope with.

SWARD: Do you think that writers need to dissociate themselves from that craziness?

MACEWEN: Certainly, if they want to get anything done. On the other hand, since they don't have the same sort of schedule as most people, then there's the freedom to come and go at will.

SWARD: Yet, there are writers who feed on the frenzy, the involvement.

MACEWEN: That's true. I suppose my involvement with the world is essentially a mystic one.

SWARD: I find something visionary in your work, that sense of seeing through, to us. Time vanishes; there's an immediate correspondence no matter how geographically or historically "remote" your subject might be.

MACEWEN: Well, I've been writing some new poems in the past month which have a fluidity that pleases me. Perhaps the strenuously paradoxical elements in some of my earlier work are settling down. Of course, when a writer is interviewed he always says he's in a new phase. And in fact he always is.

SWARD: The continuity is always there, though.

MACEWEN: Yes, but the mood changes, the stance changes. I was much more excitable in my twenties; there was a nervous energy at work. Whereas now I see that my lines in poetry are getting longer and longer. I'm not satisfied with short, breathless lines any more. It bores me to read skinny little poems. I seem to be seeking a long sustained line rather than that breathless quality.

SWARD: There's a different kind of thoughtfulness coming in.

MACEWEN: There must be. I'm more interested in bringing ideas around to completion, to see them through a cycle. I had to do this in the Lawrence poems, Lawrence being such a multiple paradox. I was faced with an interesting challenge; to present those conflicting tensions and see them through to some kind of conclusion. It wasn't enough just to state them. I think poetry has to do more than simply describe moods such as despair; there's an ethical responsibility in poetry as well. It must suggest some type of solution to the human dilemma. Art should be redeeming, in some way spiritually therapeutic. What I'm saying basically is that the artist must do something about these negative states. He has a responsibility to find meaning in them.

SWARD: Have you always felt that?

MACEWEN: Yes. I've always felt that it isn't enough to write poems about how happy or how sad I am, or for that matter about my own personal condition as such. I have to go beyond that. My own state becomes significant only when it reflects something universal.

SWARD: Don't the poems themselves allow you to do that?

MACEWEN: Yes, that's when one starts becoming instructed by one's own poetry.

SWARD: It occurred to me earlier that your exhaustive research might well replace that formal education you bypassed, deliberately.

MACEWEN: Yes, I'm self-taught. I love researching things, exercising my memory. And there are languages, of course. I studied Arabic for a time, and I'm fairly fluent in modern Greek. I find I can learn a lot more by working on my own.

SWARD: Is there a store of subjects you have, or do you reach the point where you want to write, but are without a specific theme?

MACEWEN: That would be bliss because it would mean that my mind could for a while be empty. No, it's quite the contrary. I'm afraid I'm never without a theme. It's a question of being overwhelmed by ideas. The hard work is in just choosing which one is to take precedence.

SWARD: Do you keep them inside, or do you have to write them down?

MACEWEN: Oh, both. It's never, never a question of having to look for an idea. The problem is getting rid of the excess ideas. I don't think I've ever had anything that I would call a writer's block. I don't understand the phrase, really. Yet, maybe that's because I always have one large project in the works. I keep working even when I don't feel like it. I wouldn't feel like a professional otherwise. I can understand not being able to complete a poem sometimes, but that's not writer's block.

SWARD: Do you do a lot of revision?

MACEWEN: In prose, yes. Not too much in poetry, and that's because

I write poetry much more slowly and carefully than I did before. I spend a long time on one line now, but I know it's just right when I do get it down. I'm more confident of my own voice now, and also, I usually get one line that contains the germ of the poem, and the rest follows relatively smoothly.

SWARD: Have others motivated you?

MACEWEN: When I started, I read as much as I could of modern poetry, and I suppose I was most excited by Hart Crane, who I think is a poet's poet, a very difficult, but moving poet, if you have the patience to read him. I may not feel that way now. And I guess the overall strongest influence was Yeats. Also I find, like a lot of writers, the more I write, the less I want to read. I'm a very poor reader now; I don't keep up with current books at all. Perhaps if I didn't write for a long period of time I would read more. If you look around, you'll see I have no bookshelves and no books except those I'm working with. The few books I own, I keep in trunks or drawers.

SWARD: I reviewed your adaptation of *The Trojan Women* produced by Toronto Arts Productions, a couple years back, and I remember commenting on the power of your language. Is dramatic writing beginning to interest you even more now?

MACEWEN: Yes, I think it's very exciting. Leon Major, who directed *The Trojan Women*, feels keenly that more poets should write for the theatre; it's such a natural situation for them.

SWARD: Your forthcoming play encompasses the ethnic, largely Greek, experiences of New Canadians.

MACEWEN: Well, this is a contemporary play. It's not like *The Trojan Women*. I wrote it originally as a stage play, and now Leon Major and I are turning it into a television play. It's such a different type of writing.

SWARD: What kinds of pleasure does the play give you as a writer?

MACEWEN: I enjoy drama because it's less solitary than other forms of writing. One gets to work with the actors eventually.

SWARD: I was listening to Michel Tremblay talk at a theatre conference in Montreal recently and he's just done the other thing— gone from some years of theatre writing to producing novels. For him, it was finally bliss to work alone.

MACEWEN: Yet, but I think most writers will do anything for company, given half a chance. Most writers are dying for someone to interrupt them when they're working.

SWARD: How do you deal with the loneliness?

MACEWEN: Oh, one just gets used to it. I've been writing for over twenty years now. It's not really a painful loneliness. It's a quality of life I'm accustomed to.

SWARD: For me, the loneliness appears either before or after the intensity of writing— when I come out of it and everybody's either running around, or disappearing because I haven't been there for them.

MACEWEN: But it's never a despairing loneliness.

SWARD: Unlike *The Trojan Women*, there is no mythological framework informing your current play?

MACEWEN: No, and I'm learning to write the kind of dialogue that people actually speak. It's refreshing. I'm forced to think about concrete situations and dilemmas and imagine what individuals would really say, not just how a poem about these things might sound. It's new for me.

SWARD: I wonder if this new direction will come into future work?

MACEWEN: Probably it will. Yet I'm not sure where to go with contemporary dialogue. I listen to talk in the street or wherever, and I'm always aware that people mean so much more than they say, so simple speech doesn't seem rich enough to express your inner thoughts.

SWARD: But in theatre you're lucky if you can work with a director who really understands those forces behind speech and can unleash them on stage.

MACEWEN: Yes, I think I still have to learn to accept that and understand that so much else happens to a script after it's written. I'm always fairly open to suggestions for change. But not in poetry, of course. The poem always stands alone.

Between Continuity and Difference

Daphne Marlatt interviewed by Brenda Carr

Daphne Marlatt is the author of several books of poetry, including *Steveston, How Hug a Stone,* and *Salvage,* and she is also the author of the novels *Ana Historic* and *Taken.* She lives in Victoria, B.C.

BRENDA CARR: I like to think of your life/text in process as being like Adrienne Rich's— a dance between continuity and difference. Along these lines, is there a way in which the openness of the "Black Mountain" projective poetics that allowed for translation from an American to a Canadian *Tish* context, also allows for translation to the explicitly feminist context of your writing in the 1980s?

DAPHNE MARLATT: Part of the openness of that poetic had to do with being open to proprioception, to the bio-feedback of your body in the act of composition. That's what the breath-line is supposed to be based on. So that became a ground for me to shift into a feminist bringing of the body into the act of writing. When Cixous talks about the way a woman speaks in public, how she launches all of her body into the act of speaking, that resonated for me with Olson's sense of the body's rhythms in passionately engaged thought moving the breath line. But you can't make a simple transference. Woman's body has been so repressed in our culture, fetishized on the surface but repressed deeply in terms of our actual sexuality and the force of our desire. It has been a long journey for me to come into my body, to be centred in, the *subject* of, my desire and not the object of someone else's. To develop my own sense of the line or even of how I might move through syntax to speak my own being, I had to give up trying to imitate men. And of course in those days, the early '60s, when we had just discovered the New American writing and all my mentors and models were men, it was very easy to aspire to think like a man. After all, the writers we valued, the ones who seemed to have a large "take" on the world, a political edge combined with an historical-mythical, even spiritual breadth of vision, were all men: Duncan, Olson, Creeley, Snyder, Ginsberg, Williams, Pound. Where were the women? Well, there was H.D., there was Denise Levertov, Diane di Prima, Joanne Kyger— somehow their writing was regarded as secondary because it was too personal. Even when Levertov wrote about the Viet Nam War, it was "too personal" because she was "too angry," and that got in the way of the lyric. Being a woman writer seemed to mean being always on the periphery trying to emulate men, trying to emulate their "objectivity." So the question was, how did my being a woman make a difference in my writing? A difference not peripheral but central. And if we were going to start with the body, well, my body was certainly different from Charles Olson's. So there's the notion of body and body rhythms which, I think, have been strong in my work ever since *Rings*. But there's also how you position yourself in the world. To enter the world, I mean to really take it on conceptually and feel you have as valid an analysis of what you see going on around you as any man does, is a difficult thing for a woman, perhaps the most difficult leap to make as a woman writer. And I had the benefit of a poetic that, as you say, was open, that placed me, gender aside (well, there's the problem), in an open field of composition and, in terms of ethics, set me within an environment I was interwoven with and responsible to. I think the ecological aspect of this poetic is very strong. The twinning of the language field, how you move within it, and the environmental field, how you move within that, and what your response-ability is in each case— that was a very important contribution. Now we have this notion of eco-feminism and this sense that women take responsibility for what's happening in strip mining, in the clear-cutting of forests, the polluting of our waters— this sense that women are no longer confined to the old archetypes of enclosure within a domestic space. And we're not only "urban guerrillas," to use Nicole Brossard's term in another context, but forest guerrillas, too, as the women who have gone to prison in B.C. recently to stop clear-cut logging have demonstrated. But this is happening because at last we see ourselves in responsible relation to what surrounds us, and we feel an urge to act or to write in that large relational context we're embedded in. I can see a distant link between that and the *Maximus Poems*, but it's taken many shifts and turns along the way. And that action by women is certainly not something Olson would have included in his universe. I mean the projective size of *Maximus* is definitely male.

CARR: But you would be in some ways connecting up Olson's conception of the poem as open field with that relational poetic stance?

MARLATT: Yes, but I think of that very much as Duncan's term, too— the open field. When we talk about Black Mountain poetics, we always seem to talk about Olson and Creeley. And incidentally, it was Creeley who brought the sentence alive for me in prose, the way the movement of syntax reflects the movement of consciousness in the act of perception— a kind of reflexive action. Creeley's a remarkable prose writer. But it was Duncan's line that moved me. He was really the muse-figure or mentor who gave me permission to launch into the content of my first book, *Frames*. And being a gay writer, he also validated the claiming of sexuality that is not conventional heterosexuality. The other thing about Duncan is that he took me to H.D. and H.D. became a kind of guiding intelligence along my own path of discovery. Not so much the Imagist H.D., but the H.D. of *Trilogy* and of the prose. I read the Imagist H.D. first, but the first book of hers I read that really spoke to me in the early '60s was *Bid Me to Live*. I don't remember now when I read *Trilogy*— it must have been some time in the mid-'70s— but *Trilogy* opened up what a woman could do in the long poem; it just lifted the horizon line of what was possible. The way she weaves in history, culture, mythology, her own trepidations as a woman writer, her self-doubts, it was extraordinary and very moving for me to read. And then Duncan and his sense of the opening of the field: you could shift back and forth so radically between a large and very serious poetic vision and the colloquial, the profane, sexual joking. The fluidity of these levels of language, that was very important. Olson also does this in the overall context of his writing project, but he's less fluid in the immediate and he's more deliberate, more ponderous, he takes himself more seriously in the writing. Duncan's openness to the figures of the psyche, his sense of humour, those rhythms learned from Stein, all of these felt closer to me. But I suppose it wasn't until H.D. that I came across a *woman* whose work and whose concerns as a writer seemed so much in relation to my own, even though she lived in a different period and in other countries. That she was a poet who was equally interested in prose, that she'd had a strongly Christian upbringing and was engaged in working with that, that she'd been involved in her own process of discovery through therapy, that she was a lesbian and had an ongoing relationship with Bryher—that intrigued me, although at the time I was afraid to recognize my own leanings that way. But her insistence on the feminine in all her writing, her resistance to and her continuing dialogue with the men around her, particularly Pound. Her difficulty in extricating herself, even sending him, very late in her career, a poem and saying, "Well, it might give you some pleasure to tear this apart." Astonishing, but it echoes my own situation vis à vis the men in the *Tish* scene. I felt deeply involved with what they were all expounding, not only in terms of writing but in terms of ethics, a vision of how to live. You see, that was what was so amazing about that poetic— I was going to say it involved every aspect of your life, which is not true, certainly not as true as it is of feminism, which really does involve a total re-visioning of your life. But at that age, late teens and early twenties, the change in aesthetics and values was pretty profound for me.

CARR: This leads me to think about the question of the way a woman writer situates herself in literary tradition, and perhaps I should say literary traditions. You were the only woman writer frequently cited and anthologized with the otherwise all male *Tish*-affiliated writers. As well, you've mentioned the literary patrimony fostered by the predominantly male Black Mountain precursors who, in Olson's words, saw themselves as the "sons of Pound and Williams." As a young woman writer, you seem to be indicating by what you've been saying that there was a sense of internal conflict, perhaps similar to what Adrienne Rich defines as "an unconscious fragmentation of identity" between a sense of self as woman and poet. You're already speaking about finding a place in alternate traditions via Duncan.

MARLATT: Definitely. Let me tell you about Denise Levertov. And it was through Duncan too that I got to know her work. Her presence at the 1963 conference at UBC was very important to me though I was shy about approaching her— perhaps the people who personally mean the most to us are the ones we feel most shy with. Anyway, there she was, a woman poet who gave a marvellous reading, and that was the first time I ever saw a woman hold a whole audience with the magic of her voice. I remember going to lunch with her in the cafeteria and her openness towards me as a young woman poet, and her wanting, not just to talk about writing with me, but to talk about my life with me. I remember telling her something I was having trouble with, that one of the older writers in the department, a major figure in Canadian literature, had said to me, I suppose in a moment of his own despair, "What's the use of giving a woman an education? You'll just get married and stop writing." I was about to get married then. When I relayed this to Denise, she scoffed and said, "Why, that's ridiculous. Marriage doesn't have anything to do with whether you continue to write or not. Look at me." Well, that's a totally anecdotal answer to your question. I think the fragmentation was deeply unconscious at that age. I was still imbued with that tradition of male models, and I didn't even realize consciously how much of a disparity there was, but I think probably that comment, which deeply shocked me, was the first recognition I had that women were not treated as equals to men in the seriousness of their engagement in writing. That's probably why I was so angry about it. I mean, I'm still angry about it, all these years later. Although they've been omitted from literary histories of that scene, there were other women involved in *Tish* and the Writer's Workshop then. Gladys Hindmarch was very present, and Pauline Butling was there, as well as Ginny Smith, Carol Johnson. And Maxine Gadd and Judy Copithorne were very active in the group around bill bissett and *Blewointment*. In fact, in the second phase of *Tish*, which nobody remembers, when a group of us who were younger took over the magazine after the others had left, there was more of a cross-over with the *Blewointment* group and we were publishing Maxine's poetry and Judy's. So I didn't feel, at the time, like I was the only one, though I did feel a certain resistance to the dominance of the men. It was the men who really defined the terms of the prevailing aesthetic at the writing workshops, which was really the collective activity behind *Tish*. It's only the filter of history that says I'm the lone woman, and it overlooks the fact that Gladys, who was involved from the beginning, has continued to write, continued to publish. Actually, my writing companionship with Fred and George and Gladys as well as with Maxine and Judy didn't really begin until after *Tish* was over and I had moved back to Vancouver. By then I had published two books and established myself as a writer. You see, in the *Tish* days there was quite a disparity in age. When I first met Frank, with whom I did have a sort of companionship for a while then, and Fred, George, Jamie, Lionel, I was only an undergraduate in my first year while they were all graduate students.

CARR: You've already been pointing to the fact that the long poem is a very important genre for you, as it was for many of the other *Tish*-affiliated writers and their Black Mountain predecessors. In fact, your *Steveston* has been frequently compared with Olson's *Maximus Poems* and Williams' *Paterson*. Michael Bernstein, a theorist of the long poem, asserts that such works tell the "tale of the tribe." Is there a way in which your writing in its dance between long poem and autobiography does not tell the tale of the tribe, but rather works to subvert the objective and "universal" (we could say, implicitly male) frames of the genre in terms of content, voice, and formal strategies?

MARLATT: Well, first of all, who is the tribe? Louky Bersianik, in the paper she gave at the Women and Words Conference in 1983, did a brilliant critique of the masculinism of the anthropological assumptions bound up in the notion of tribe. The Steveston work that Robert (Minden) and I did involved coming to some understanding of that. In the beginning, when we were doing the aural history project with Maya (Koizumi) and Rex (Weyler), we all approached Steveston as a fishing community. Fishing is done by the men. Only gradually did it become apparent to some of us that we also needed to talk to the women— I mean, this was getting very one-sided. Later, when Robert and I were working on our own on *Steveston*, we talked about how Steveston's women seemed invisible and I realized that what I wanted to make surface through the obvious ring of that town's fishing activity were the women, the women you didn't see on the streets, you didn't see on the docks because they were at home, or they were in the cannery. In the hospital poem, which is based on an old photograph of the first community hospital in Steveston and is a poem about a woman either dying or giving birth, I began to realize that the movement of the river out towards the sea, where it disappears, was a movement into the invisible that had to do with birthing and dying, and that in fact the two were metaphors of each other. So that which remained invisible and unspoken, women's part in the town, was also crucial— just as the movement of the river, which I was fascinated by and was trying to imitate in the rhythms of the poem, was not just background. Much later when I was working on *Touch to My Tongue* and heard the rhythms moving like the rhythms in *Steveston* I realized they were orgasmic. I think I got very close to realizing that in the hospital poem, but there was something in the way and that was the original concept of the project, that it was a fishing town, that it was the men's activity that was of interest. But throughout that book I think I was writing my way to a reversal of that focus, a sort of figure/ground reversal. This business of what becomes figure and what becomes ground is very fascinating to me. It's part of the ecological vision in *Steveston*, trying to shift that ground which is usually background for the figure so it becomes foreground. The shift in values that's involved is also what feminism is about. But to get back to your question about the autobiographical, yes, the voice in most of my work is subjective and individual rather than universal. It's marked by my gender as well as my history, class, national identity, race, all those things. *Steveston* has often been called a documentary but the writing doesn't assume that there is an unmediated objective position. I put myself in there, recording all the sexual baggage I carried as a woman on the dock. I suppose that continues in a different way in *How Hug a Stone* because I'm there as a woman in a foreign country which is not a foreign country. There's that twist running through it, that I'm claiming it and, at the same time, feeling very alienated from it, which is probably the classic emigrant position towards the country of origin. It's not really an origin in my case, it never was, though all the family stories pretended that it was, so I went back with that expectation. So there's this constant fracturing, just as there is in the mother/daughter duality, being both a daughter and a mother at the same time, the no-longer-English mother of a Canadian son who is fascinated by the foreignness of the English. A universal voice can't admit this kind of fracturing, or those kinds of differences. The universal wants to pretend difference doesn't exist.

CARR: You've already indicated that Olson's projective poetics is rooted in his objectivist stance that proposes decentering the human subject and revaluing all the forms of life and experience. You really adapt this notion to the ecological vision that you've conceptualized in *Steveston* where you bring forward the image of the net or the web as a metaphor of this sense of interconnection between human life and all life forms in the environment. There seems to be a resonance between your ecological stance and your poetics, where you talk, for example in *What Matters*, about the "ecological movement of words." Has this vision of life and language that you were formulating in your early work been carried along and adapted to your present feminist poetics?

MARLATT: Well, this brings up figure and ground in a different way. I think that where I was angry at the foregrounding of capitalist values and human life concerns at the expense of other forms of life, that anger then focussed on the foregrounding of patriarchal male values and concerns at the expense of female being and a female ethos that tends to be more relational and contextually aware. This shift meant that I was suddenly writing from the margin. As soon as you try to write from the margin versus the centre, so that the margin is seen from the centre of its own values, then you're open to the attack that you're simply trying to reverse the hierarchy and make this *the* centre. This is a trap of binary thinking, which is always hierarchical. It says there has to be an either/or and it can't get to that place of both/and. Cixous and Irigaray have written about this. The either/or seems to be actually embedded in the definitional activity of our language. As a poet, and even more intensively as a feminist writer, I am mostly having to resist that, to work against it. The question is, how to get to a multivalency of meaning based on equivalency without losing meaning altogether? Meaning is so rooted in current usage, which itself is so freighted with patriarchal value. I can't ignore that, it's a given. But I can work to subvert it, to undermine it, and that's where all the different kinds of wordplay come into effect, from deconstructing words to inventing new ones, to using etymology as another variant on meaning. People seem to misunderstand my use of etymology and accuse it of being a validation of "the true literal meaning" of the word. That's very far from what I'm doing which is much more playful than that. It's a way of calling up an absolutely departed from or an ignored and forgotten meaning and recycling it as a variant slant on, a new fracture of, the current meaning, which after all still stands, though it's now no longer dominant. It's a form of polysemy.

CARR: In recent writing, like *Touch to My Tongue*, you recycle the ecological imagery of *Steveston*, especially that of the Fraser River, so that it becomes an embodiment of your experience of woman-to-woman eroticism. It is possible to see this aspect of your work as sliding towards the patriarchal essentialist trap that reduces woman to body/sexuality, erases differences between women, conflates woman with nature, and ultimately leaves women outside of culture and cultural production. In an interview with Janice Williamson, you indicate that you see your use of this imagery as a self-conscious recuperation, a gesture of double decolonization of what has been traditionally devalued as "feminine." Is this eco-feminist position still a necessary corrective to our world that is sometimes seen as "post-colonial" (and I might add "post-feminist")?

MARLATT: Our world certainly isn't post-colonial or post-feminist. And presuming to speak from a "post" position just blinds us to the fact that things haven't really changed all that much. As for the essentialist position, the problem is that when women have been reduced in the dominant culture from being subjects in our own right to being objects of male desire, then it becomes necessary to try to "deculturate" ourselves in order to imagine what it could be like for us to be acculturated otherwise in a woman-affirming culture. There are various images for this: the "wild zone," the "Amazon," and so on. What it comes down to in *Touch* is that I'm speaking from within a lesbian culture that is a sub-culture within the patriarchal culture we're all embroiled with. And lesbian culture tries to do something which, as Nicole Brossard has said, is unimaginable from within the dominant culture. We try to imagine that fullness of who we might be outside of patriarchal reference. Women have historically been defined in reference to men. So to imagine ourselves not in reference to them but in reference to ourselves, our own strengths, our own being, our own beauty, is almost unimaginable. It means seeing everything in a different light, it means seeing yourself in relation to what goes on around you in a new context. That contextual shift is dramatically different and it's hard to convey in the forms and language we have inherited, which are freighted so much the other way. To make present what has been erased— our bodies, our desire, our self-definition, and how that breaches the symbolic, our solidarity with other women at a level that can meet our differences, our reciprocity with other forms of life— so much that we are now trying to bring out of the unspeakable: this can only be seen as reductive if the large contextual shift it involves is ignored. Which means ignoring what we start off with, what Teresa de Lauretis, translating a term from the Italian feminists, calls, "originary difference." To say that this leaves women outside of culture is to speak from within patriarchal ground, because it suggests that there is only one recognizable culture, the dominant patriarchal one, and it denies the radically new culture being born in that contextual shift. It's hard to recognize this culture because it isn't monolithic or singular. It's more like an area of response between different oppressed or minority cultures, and the women's movement is just beginning to work out the kind of response required in any truly reciprocal condition where the differences between women of colour and white women, and between lesbian women and heterosexual women, to name only two of a number of differences, make communication and trust very different.

CARR: Self-consciously writing from the margins, claiming them, creating them as a "wild zone" where the differences resonate/vibrate between and among women and other oppressed groups, ultimately connects back to a reframing of Olson's notion of valuing the "local" in a feminist context.

MARLATT: I do have my feet in the west coast. It was part of my original immigrant passion for the place, which I found validated in Olson's poetic. But feminism does reframe it. It's not such a big jump to see strip-mining, clear-cut logging, drift-netting as all forms of colonial domination. To see the connection between the exploitation of other species and the exploitation of women is not to reduce women to nature. That's exactly what patriarchal thought does. Seeing the ways in which we are connected to other forms of life, to other races, other classes, is to work against the domination of one over all the others. The vision feminism embodies, it seems to me, is relational, promoting an equivalency of needs, not the privileging of one set.

CARR: In *Salvage*, you recollect poems from the *Steveston* period and rewrite them. One of the meanings of the word "salvage" is "sophistical evasion." Is there a way in which an eco-feminist poetics as a gesture of "salvage" in language need not be contextualized within a rigid essentialist categorization of gender?

MARLATT: Well, that meaning surprises me. I've been working on the sense of salvage as "something extracted (as from wreckage, ruins, or rubbish) as valuable," and it seems to me that this kind of salvaging involves revaluing in the way that we've just been talking about, re-visioning (I do use Adrienne Rich's term for it), and neither of those acts seems to participate in sophistry. In fact, they're essential for a woman's coming to speak out of her hitherto absent body, absent desire, and muted voice within a public context. To do this she has to valorize the ground out of which she speaks. Which means working for a really drastic change in our culture. Working for change is what makes feminism different from postmodernism, I learned from the *Tish* days. Even though there's a continuity with some of those strategies, I'm using them for different ends now. As Linda Hutcheon says in her article in *Tessera* 7, postmodernism, although it critiques the master narratives of our culture, the institutions and the codes, still ends up being complicit with them because it has no program for change. A program for change means valorizing a difference, and as soon as you valorize a difference you're moving out of postmodernist deconstruction into a position of, as she says, belief or trust in a certain metanarrative. It's a difference at such a basic level that I think it's often been overlooked, but it's a difference that leads to a radical shift in world view.

CARR: I was thinking of "sophistical evasion" as playful possibility. What about the potential of salvage as a baffle, a feint, a dodge, a side-step game with cultural definitions? I am thinking of "s," the female protagonist of your *Character*, of Roland Barthes' notion of character in *S/Z*, where the character shows up in different guises/disguises at the multiple entrances of the labyrinthine text. If the sophists were known for their "adroit, subtle and allegedly specious reasoning" (as in tending to deceive or mislead), this resonates with the playful evasion of the female subject of the feminist text, as well as with the playful dance, the shimmer of meanings of the text as subject, and links up, too, with the irrational of your "Musing with Mothertongue" in subversion of patriarchal reason.

MARLATT: What a wonderful inversion. Why *not* reclaim "sophistry" in order to take an alternate approach to representation? The "dodge" is what's required when we find ourselves up against our absence in patriarchal definition, even as we assert our difference from it, not to mention our differences within it. And then there's "sapphistry," which might stand for another order of reason altogether.

The Poem Comes out of the Machine

Erin Mouré interviewed by Beverley Daurio

Erin Mouré is the author of eight books of poetry, including *Furious, Search Procedures,* and *The Green Word (Selected Poems, 1973-1992).* Her most recent book is *A Frame of the Book.*

Some years ago, poet Erin Mouré was asked by the TVOntario literary program, *Imprint*, to make a poetry video. In Erin's video, a computer printer chugs and chugs. Mouré sits on a chair, and the poem comes out of the machine. She leans forward and reads three or four pages, glancing up now and then at the camera. The room is plain, with cream walls; perhaps it is her writing room, perhaps not. The writing is beautiful, but neither her voice— caramel, steel and somehow indefatigably optimistic— nor her demeanour are seduced by that beauty. The camera does not move; there are no concessions to the illusions of television. Mouré is working, that much is clear; what is clearer is that she is entirely skeptical about the business of being on screen.

My impression of Mouré as skeptical about how information is presented in the media is supported by her own poetry and essays. It is also clear in interviews with her— Erin once affectionately suggested that an interviewer question a pancake instead of her. With this skepticism in mind, I hesitantly compiled some "facts" about her:

Erin Claire Mouré was born in 1955, in Calgary, Alberta. She is the author of several books of poetry. The first of these books, *Empire, York Street,* published when Mouré was 24 years old, was nominated for a Governor General's Award for Poetry.

Mouré lives in Montreal, not terribly far from McGill University, The Main (rue St. Laurent), and café-dotted rue St. Denis. She does not smoke. Employed as Senior Officer, Customer

Relations and Employee Communications at VIA Rail, Mouré lifts weights on a regular basis, rises weekdays at 5 a.m. and retires at 9 p.m. She prefers to write first thing in the morning.

Erin Mouré won the Governor General's Award for Poetry for *Furious* in 1988, and the QSPELL Award in 1990, for *WSW (West South West)*.

Erin Mouré has been prescient. These are the final lines from *Empire, York Street*:

> In my country, the politicians talk
> of referenda. They do not believe, & while they are not believing
> the bones will break loose,
> triumphant, singing like birds.

Baldly presented, my "facts" about Erin Mouré display their inadequacy as a way of discovering Erin to the reader. As Mouré said in *WSW* (*West South West*), "The speech is the writer's speech and each word of the writer robs the witnessed of their own voice, muting them." Nor is Mouré's admonishment about voice part of a lecture; about her own work, she wrote: "only my assumptions, only the arrogance of Erin Mouré made into the poem..."

Mouré is not sympathetic to the idea that exposing bits of her life might help to sell books:

> [Personal details] focus on the person, not the work. I am more complicated than the details. And more irrelevant than the work... too many personal details are just clutter. It's all a construct anyhow, out of context. I would like the focus to be on writing, the act I love. Where I am just one small working voice. That's enough.

Mouré's poetry is at the same time deeply personal— though not in the confessional sense— and epic in scope. Her poetry *is* her public expression, not a representation of her *self*. Her self, she insists, is material: a person who gets up early and goes to work at VIA Rail on Monday mornings, who laughs and cooks for friends. Her being, like anyone's, cannot be represented by the haphazard connect-the-dots approach of written biography.

There are writers whose resistance to celebrity— J.D. Salinger and Thomas Pynchon come to mind— seems an idiosyncratic aspect of character, a struggle for privacy which is untheoretical and basically self-protective. Mouré's resistance is different, inspired by her rigorous questioning of and responsibility toward speech. But:

> "Responsible" not to the civic order and its maintenance, but to the "polis" which is people as a civic organism/unity. When the civic order is a) killing us, and b) excluding many of us and constructing all of us, responsibility to the "polis" means defying that. Maintenance of the civic order is the political subtext to naming some work "difficult." I prefer "poses difficult questions."

Mouré is open and forthcoming about herself, and often funny and ironic. But her consciousness of the "constructed" nature of any representation of the real throws a sentence like "in person, Mouré is lively and tall, with chin-length brown hair and a quick, intelligent gaze" back on itself. I can't "represent" *Erin* here; I can only construct an unreal image of her, quote her answer to, for instance, a question about the current state of Canadian culture:

> Artists finance/subsidize with our lives the production of art, and have had some considerable help with the presentation of it. Now the help is a lot less, and when this happens, the artists are left to subsidize the presentation of art as well. It's like having a kid, when the father is too tired, *écouré*, fed up, the mother still must summon the energy and attentiveness to raise the child.

The presentation is essential; it provides a ground, a meeting-place, a way for ideas to be exchanged, heard. With it, art develops, people find it. Without that presentation, art can become hidden, clandestine, growth slows. The polis shrivels. This is happening, will happen. It will be more difficult for society as a whole to resist the trans-national Americanization and commodification of culture, when they are less able to hear us, know about those of us whose lives are a resistance to that.

The roots of Mouré's thoughtful iconoclasm are eminently interesting. I suggested to Erin that details about her early life might be helpful to a young woman, for example, struggling to define herself, especially in view of Erin's statement that when she was young "there just weren't enough images or role models," and she answered several questions about her youthful experiences with public and social institutions:

ON PUBLIC SCHOOL:

"I liked: learning amazing things, reading, arithmetic. Disliked: being cowed by the arbitrary exercise of power, and the very narrow order that was drilled into us. *Sit down, don't look out the window, stay on the same page.* These were the real lessons. Of course I couldn't put it in those words at the age of five or six. It was just confusing. Blows could come from anywhere."

BRIEFLY, ON FAMILY:

"My name is Spanish, Galician. I'm 'Heinz 57' but mostly descended from people whose land was always run by someone else.

"My father read to us; we didn't have much at home but we were always at the library. Reading was valued. Education was valued; if you could get it, maybe you wouldn't have to work at some awful jobs. Material goods were not valued... there weren't any, but they weren't coveted, either."

ON BECOMING A FEMINIST:

"My father sent my brothers outside to cut the lawn and work in the yard, and I had to stay in and wash the dishes. Did I cry! My brothers didn't defend me one little bit (the alternative for them was the dishes, you see). I had to stir up all the shit, solo. I had two adults arguing with me. The division of duties didn't stick, though. Noone could give me a reason that held up. My mother understood; her heart wasn't in the argument."

ON HIGH SCHOOL:

"Too much 'norming,' and the ache of not fitting in and absolutely not knowing why, or what alternative there might be. There were teachers who encouraged reading... Earlier than high school, junior high, there was [poet] Claire Harris, who really made me think about language, how it is put together, its flexibility and sinew, the way it works as a body, structures thought. She made us read Shakespeare, and write compositions, write, write, write. The act itself was of value. I still have the report card where she told me I wasn't working hard enough, wasn't working to expand the limits of my capability, I guess."

Erin left the two universities she attended, each for about a year: "I was restless; there wasn't enough range. Undergraduates were fodder." And then she went to work, in factories, on the trains: "I had to find some way to support myself. I did what I felt was possible."

Asked how she came to understand herself to be lesbian, Erin responds: "The idea of 'understanding myself' makes me howl. It's oxymoronic. But to answer: what a long ache I went through. No one wants to be castigated, or to be faced with the homophobia of others. Or, for that matter, to face one's own homophobia... it took me years even to find a name for what I felt."

Only a few years after Mouré left Calgary, her first book was published. "I just wrote... early on I had this idea that I would try to keep three submissions in the mail at all times. That was the goal. When something came back, I'd examine it critically to see if it still looked neat, then ship it out again. Jim Polk at Anansi asked for my first book. I don't think I've learned the business of publishing, though. I think books are too claustrophobic for poetry, anyhow."

Mouré's resistance to iconography— "I don't want to be some big poet"— raises numerous issues, including the question of reportage as a mediator of and distraction from actual experience. To what degree do we lose the depth and capacity of our own senses when we are constantly bombarded with surface constructs of people we have not met as simple and knowable? Ought the subject of reportage to be willing, for example, to scatter quick answers to questions that otherwise required years of concentration, perhaps, simply to formulate, never mind answer, when the poetry, the result of those years of work is available for consultation?

Many years ago now, Mouré worked on the trains for VIA. Could a request to describe her experience of the trains elicit a more evocative response than this?:

That this is what i chose. To watch
years step from the station into light:
always to the tracks, steady as a dream.
Or that shaken.
The rest leaving or returning, & me
stopped by the waiting steel.
...
Not to regret, even a little.
No. I came to this, & agreed, & it took me.
Holds me yet.

    (from "what the station agent never says,"
Empire, York Street)

Or:

> I feel I am in the world & there is no god in it with me.
> ...
> He says there are glasses as big as women filled with rye & he wants
> to marry one.
> This is what I listen to, no wonder
> I can't sleep.
>   (from "Tricks," *Wanted Alive*)

Or:

> Don't be afraid of thinking
> otherwise. All poems have
> their own amazing order,
> by which we decode
> "the author's intention."
>   (from "Order, or Red Ends: Order 4," *WSW*)

Out of context snippets from Erin's substantial body of work
cannot do that work justice: Mouré's vision ranges over vast, previously uncharted, mysterious ground, plundering philosophy, Der-
ridian theory, current events— among thousands of other things— and
echoing (not replicating) many voices:

> **As if all voice came out of the self! The big "me!" I think women,
> who are, both historically and currently, in a de-authorized
> position vis a vis speech (in the social context, where we still
> lack authority unless we assume it in the same way as men)
> absorb, conflate, hear the speech of others mixed in with our
> own words, hear more of a community of voices, voices echoing
> other bits of voices that we retain as synaptic triggers in the**

head. No one voice being "self-present" or indicating self-presence.

The appearance of Mouré's poetry on the page has changed little over the years, and she has been involved in the typesetting of several of her books. Mouré says: "It's important to me. You're dealing with the alphabet, and with the visual representation of the lungs, of breath. I myself have drawn the alphabet over and over. Out of respect."

What *has* changed is the method of construction of her books. Her early works— *Empire, York Street, Wanted Alive* and *Domestic Fuel*— are collections— if internally interrelated and coherently organized collections— of discrete poems. In them, Mouré's lasting preoccupations are present— war, her own concrete experience, politics, justice, women, metaphysics, the sacred— as also occur the precursors to her later work, long poems like "Riel: In the Season of his Birth," as well as suites and sequences. The language is energetic, exploratory, disciplined, and wild, the images strikingly true and hammeringly memorable. With *Furious*, however, comes both a statement of aesthetic intention, "The Acts," and a different approach:

I guess with *Furious* I started to see the "book" (the illusory book, not the published object) as the unit of production, as it were. The illusory book is the one I am writing into, am honouring. It is a state of presence, a state of belief, even.

The complex aesthetic revealed in *Furious*, which reads in part— "It isn't that to change the weight and force of English will *necessarily* make women's speaking possible. But to move the force in any language, create a slippage, *even for a moment...* to decentre the 'thing,' unmask the relation"— is fulfilled in the novel-like works *WSW* and *Sheepish Beauty, Civilian Love*, daring, uncompromising maps of thought in words:

Some want poetry to comfort and nourish their assumptions, not abrade them. I have to listen and respect the language, the words; I can't be responsible for making things easy on the reader... You can't read all poetry like you read the *Globe & Mail*... some of it is so rich that one line is enough for a century. [*Sheepish Beauty, Civilian Love*, is based on one line from Lorca, "O, how the wheat is tender."] Too much gets crammed into books; you have to adjust and read a bit at a time. Then get up and wash your face in cold water. And feel your way along the edge you have come to."

Asked directly for her opinion of author profiles, Mouré says:

They're only good if they help people to see themselves. The author is an invention, a woman bearing a glass plate who crashes in the doorway. If an author falls in the forest, does she make a sound? What is important is that people can be truly present to themselves. For this, you need others, a web of others, of impulses, touches, glances, words, emotions, pulls, tellurgic forces, symptoms, atoms, fuel explosions, inferences, motions, and laughter.

A reader searching for Erin Mouré in these pages is bound to be as frustrated as I am here, trying to convey the allure and power of the metaphysical landscape of her books— especially *Furious, WSW,* and *Sheepish Beauty, Civilian Love*— without being reductive. As Janet Malcolm said in her recent *New Yorker* examination of the Sylvia Plath biographies, "We must always take... the poet's word, just as we are almost always free to doubt the... journalist's." Simply, Erin Mouré is at home in Montreal. And her word is in her magical, questioning, intensely liberating poetry. Any reader can find her there.

Entranced

P.K. Page interviewed by Lucy Bashford and Jay Ruzesky

Since her first collection of poetry, *As Ten as Twenty*, was published in 1944, P.K. Page has been an important voice in Canadian poetry. She has been the recipient of many honours, including the Governor General's Award.

Hologram: A Book of Glosas (Brick Books, 1994), *The Hidden Room: Collected Poems* (Porcupine's Quill, 1997) and *Compass Rose* (Instituto Italiano di Cultura, 1998) are her most recent books. A special issue of *The Malahat Review* that celebrates P.K. and her work was published on the occasion of her eightieth birthday in the winter of 1996.

In addition to the poetry for which she is probably best known, she has written a non-fiction memoir, *Brazilian Journal*, a collection of fiction, *The Sun and the Moon and Other Fictions*, and three books for children, *The Travelling Musicians*, *A Flask of Sea Water*, and *The Goat That Flew*. She is also a visual artist whose work is in the National Gallery of Canada in Ottawa and in the Art Gallery of Ontario in Toronto.

LUCY BASHFORD & JAY RUZESKY: In the introduction to *Hologram* you explain what a glosa is and you mention the difference between "affinity for" and "influence."

P.K. PAGE: I think the idea of finding one's voice is a false construct. It's like developing a personality or something. You have one. It's there.

BASHFORD & RUZESKY: I like your analogy of birds brought up in isolation. They take from the songs of others to complete their species–song.

PAGE: It's a fascinating analogy, isn't it? I read it in an article in the *New Yorker* and it seems to apply in many areas. What could you learn in isolation? Not much.

BASHFORD & RUZESKY: But what you would take coming out of isolation is what was already yours.

PAGE: We're not thieves. The voice is innate, if undeveloped.

BASHFORD & RUZESKY: Doris Lessing suggests that writers are a kind of organism, that we are connected by what we do. It struck me as I was reading the glosas, that in this form you...

PAGE: ...marry another writer.

BASHFORD & RUZESKY: Yes. Through the text, part of the writer becomes part of us. The connection that this form makes seems profound. Not only are you making the connection that usually occurs when you read and write, and have an affinity for someone, but you link with them and it's more like the two of you sitting down and writing together. You begin so obviously with their words...

PAGE: ...and their rhythm to some extent rubs off on you. Not entirely, but to some extent. It's a funny feeling of intimacy when you're working with someone else's lines. Lessing's idea that poets are all one being, as are all people of any similar discipline, fascinated me, and I think that there is some very great truth in it. It's a very funny experience to use other people's lines. It's more than just writing a poem. It's merging. There were times when I wondered if I was just doing imitation Stevens or imitation Bishop.

BASHFORD & RUZESKY: You are merging and yet you are an individual at the same time. It's clear reading through *Hologram* that it's your book and these are your poems, and they're you.

PAGE: Well, some of my best lines are not mine. I have to accept that. It was interesting to allow someone else's line to overshadow me. I don't mean that they can't and don't frequently, but when you juxtapose them it is quite obvious and you have to be prepared to say, "All right, I'll take a back seat. That is the best line."

BASHFORD & RUZESKY: Are you thinking of one in particular?

PAGE: The Graves, actually. That extraordinary line of his: "Nor for the tall, eventual catafalque." I could never have dreamed that up in a hundred-thousand years.

BASHFORD & RUZESKY: That could easily be you!

PAGE: Of course, you don't pick the four lines, do you, unless there's some strong affinity.

BASHFORD & RUZESKY: Your work is *your* path. And it seems that there are certain elements that have been there for you for a long time. In *Hologram* there are major insights. It's very powerful. In an essay that you wrote in 1970, "Traveller, Conjuror, Journeyman," [*The Glass Air*] you say that the "struggle is to fit the "made" to the "sensed" in such a way that the whole can occupy a world larger than the one I normally inhabit. This process involves scale. Poem or painting is by-product." The process is larger than the product of the poem. It's something you may not be able to see as clearly as someone outside of a book like *Hologram*, but the poems indicate a larger process going on behind the work.

PAGE: I had a period of quite astonishing clarity when I wrote that essay. I had, for a short time, a breakthrough into another understanding. It didn't last, but I have the residue of it still. I think I've always realized how little we know and had a sense that perhaps what we are seeing is the first layer of something more. But I can't articulate it because it belongs to another life, not the life of the senses.

BASHFORD & RUZESKY: There's a mystical element in your poems, a visionary quality. Do you know where they come from?

PAGE: I haven't any idea. But I do think that when I'm very concentrated in a poem, and I am more concentrated writing a set form than writing free verse— the focus is more intense. It's a very narrow focus but it isn't a shallow focus. When people ask me if I meditate, I say, "No, I don't." But possibly I do meditate. Perhaps when I'm writing I'm meditating.

BASHFORD & RUZESKY: Is art an avenue into some more mystical place for you? What is it that opens doors? It's an odd thing to do to sit in a room alone and write.

PAGE: Some people would say it's nothing more than a form of egotism. That you think what you have to offer is so bloody important that you're prepared to shut yourself up and do it at the expense of all around you. Look at Rilke, who begged his life through in order to write. And I've known other writers who thought that they should be kept, that being a poet was enough. Clearly it can be a form of ego. But in the case of Rilke, thank god for it. Although I don't think it was ego with him.

And I've never felt it was ego with me. I don't see how anyone can get puffed up about how great they are because it seems to me that the artist is a channel. And I suppose the purer the channel— and by that I don't mean saintly but clearer— the clearer the channel the clearer what comes through. It never occurs to me that it has much to do with me and it never has. It doesn't matter whether it's a bad poem or a good poem. So I don't think it is ego. It's a process. And I'm never terribly interested in the thing when it's finished. People say, "Oh, aren't you thrilled to have the book in your hands?" The book is the by-product, the evidence of the fact that a lot of stuff went on.

I think in our age the artists have let us down very badly. And when I say artists I mean whoever the creative members of society are. I include myself in this. With some exceptions, of course, I feel we have lost our sense of scale. I don't know we seem as stuck in the "material" as any businessman.

BASHFORD & RUZESKY: We've been forced into making ourselves a "business." We're referred to as cultural industries. The tax system, all of that makes you start to think about it in a different way. We don't really have time to look *in* and beyond.

PAGE: Do we know how to get in? When you think of fiction today, there isn't much that has an extra dimension. There is some but much seems to have, in fact, anticipated the strictures imposed by voice appropriation and applied them widely. It presents too narrow a view and is not dissimilar to the confessional phase in poetry. I feel that until you can reach beyond the self, you haven't a great deal to say. It's as if we have taken a backwards step although maybe, for some unknown reason, we had to.

BASHFORD & RUZESKY: There's a connection between the economy and creativity.

PAGE: Writing poetry was never my livelihood. It was always something quite apart. I think I was lucky in that I grew up in a golden era. When we started *Preview* in Montreal in the '40s, we didn't have any money. There were no grants. Each of us put five dollars in the pot. For me that was a lot of money. I was earning eighty dollars a month. We cobbled the magazine together ourselves, very clumsily. I did most of the typing, and I was a bad typist. If any of us wrote something good, the others were always quick to say so and genuinely pleased. We felt it lifted the whole level for everybody, that it was like pouring sugar in tea. The whole of the cup was sweetened by it.

I still feel my heart lift when I read something good and I want to tell the writer. But it's different today from the '40s. Some other element seems to have crept into the world. People are more wrangly and I hate it. But I must admit I don't like it if someone I think is a bad writer gets a lot of praise.

BASHFORD & RUZESKY: But if that same person writes something brilliant...

PAGE: I honestly think I am pleased. It's the work, not the personality that matters.

BASHFORD & RUZESKY: You talk about recapturing and remembering. I'm wondering if recapturing might go beyond childhood memories to before we were born.

PAGE: I think it's a possibility. Just as I think it's a possibility that we may have chosen our parents and where we landed on earth. Because we measure time linearly, we get locked into it. But there is another time that has nothing to do with linear time and I think I have known about it since I was quite young.

BASHFORD & RUZESKY: In a bookstore I saw a section called "miscellaneous spirituality" and I thought that would be a good shelf for you. There is a solid spiritual centre in your work that I wouldn't trace to any particular place. Sufism... but even that is a non-religion.

PAGE: Actually it claims to be the inner part or essence of every religion. It is also a body of knowledge which has been enormously enriching to me.

BASHFORD & RUZESKY: In another essay you say you'd like to be a magician. Part of being a magician is being observant so you can do things other people won't notice. There's a thin line between a visionary quality and a magical quality because magicians as we know them don't do real magic.

PAGE: I don't know that I'd say that I want to be a magician today. There's quite a lot of deception in it. The Sufis say that miracles do not fly in the face of laws. They only fly in the face of laws that we, at this stage, know of. Any miracle is part of a logical or illogical construct but it isn't breaking laws, it's just in tune with higher laws that we can't possibly imagine. I wouldn't mind getting in touch with those higher laws.

BASHFORD & RUZESKY: I think that's what you're doing. *Hologram* is a powerful book because through your search you've reached some point where you're connected to something not everyone is. It's inspiring. There's a quotation at the back of Tim Lilburn's book, *Moosewood Sandhills*, from Gregory of Nysa, who says that "the desire to see God, is a vision of God." That's something that makes sense in terms of your work. Knowing that there are other places to go is a way of being there.

PAGE: That's a good quotation.

BASHFORD & RUZESKY: In the 1970 essay you ask the question, "What am I trying to do with my writing?" and the answer is "play" with a question mark. Are you still playing?

PAGE: I think so. It's very serious play. I get such pleasure out of just playing with the way words rhyme or don't rhyme. You know play can be intensely serious when you see a child sitting on the floor playing with bits of paper and an old tin can. With children it's almost as if they're in touch with another dimension.

BASHFORD & RUZESKY: And why do we lose that?

PAGE: Well, I suppose one has to get on with some very practical things in life. There are the dishes in the sink and they have to be done. There's all that business of keeping yourself clean and feeding yourself. Idries Shah, a Sufi teacher, says that once upon a time people played with toys. Now toys play with people. We seem to have allowed this material world to manipulate us, to take us over.

BASHFORD & RUZESKY: What was it like to go back over a life's work and have it collected in *The Hidden Room*? Were there any surprises?

PAGE: I don't think any real surprises. Although some of my very early work which didn't go into *The Hidden Room* surprised me. My reach so exceeded my grasp. I was astonished to see what I was reaching for and failing to deliver because of inexperience and ineptitude.

There was a very long poem about the sea as seen through the eyes of a sunbather on the beach and a fisherman who was coping with it as a reality. It surprised me because I wrote it when I was young and reaching out for something quite big and... impossible.

Some of the surprises were the poems that Stan Dragland included. I had put myself in Stan's hands pretty well, but retained the right to argue or dispute. Some of the early surrealist poetry I think I wouldn't have chosen myself.

BASHFORD & RUZESKY: There have been a number of comments about the ordering of *The Hidden Room*. People are troubled by the fact that it's not ordered chronologically. What do you think of that?

PAGE: I think first about the people who object to it. I think they've been academicized to death. Many academics think chronologically, but is it not possible for a body of work to have an organic whole that's not necessarily chronological? I think Stan found that organic whole.

There is a related subject— one that I argued about repeatedly with Dorothy Livesay. She insisted that you shouldn't revise an early poem at a later date. My position was— and is— that it depends upon what you are trying to do. If you are trying to write the best poem you are capable of, then you can and must. My poetry, after all, is not very autobiographical.

BASHFORD & RUZESKY: Was there a lot of revision, then, for this book?

PAGE: Very little, really. But I could have revised. It's my work!

BASHFORD & RUZESKY: You must have gone through chrono-logically when you were gathering the poems together for *The Hidden*

Room. That's not something that one often does. How did it feel to go back?

PAGE: I could see very clearly how pelted with images I was when I was young. And then when I reached the point where I realized how little control I had over those images, I addressed the problem in the poem, "After Rain." I wasn't quite as pelted with images after that. The act of writing came through a slightly different filter. I had made a conscious choice and in doing that, I both gained and lost. I lost a certain spontaneity perhaps. I was also interested to see how extraordinarily romantic I was— romantic and idealistic.

BASHFORD & RUZESKY: Do you see big changes in your work? I can open the book anywhere and they seem like P.K. Page poems. The voice hasn't changed that much. Do you see that, too?

PAGE: There's a certain ground, to use a musical term, that goes through it all. I think some of my rhythms were more interesting when I was young than they are now. Like this poem, "The Crow", which I wrote when I was really quite young:

> by the wave rising
> by the wave breaking
> high to low
> by the wave riding the air
> sweeping the high air low...

I don't think I could write that way now. I'm not talking about content, but my rhythmic form was more varied. Iambic has left its heavy foot on me, its elephant foot.

One of the things that emerges from *The Hidden Room* is that even when I was young I wasn't writing about myself very much. It's one of the complaints I get now; that my poetry is too impersonal. And yet it always was. I was looking out. I was looking at the man with one small hand, or the old man in the garden, or the stenographers and typists. It wasn't often that I was looking at myself, although I suppose in some sense I *was* the man with the small hand, the old man in the garden, etc., etc.

BASHFORD & RUZESKY: Was that a part of the time?

PAGE: Oh, probably. The objective-correlative of Eliot was my credo, more or less, and the confessional poets hadn't hit the fan yet; it was a different period. And yet at the same time I think of Patrick Anderson, whose work was very personal.

But I am an observer, a watcher— always have been. There was a man in Ottawa who used to call me the "Seeing-Eye Bitch." He wasn't being rude about my being bitchy. He was a dog man. He said "one has to be very careful around you because you see everything." And I did. At that period in my life I was *very* observant. It wasn't critical observation; it was camera. And if you are looking out, then you write about what you see.

I had been flung from the protected world in which I grew up to Montreal in wartime— a culture of two languages and sophisticated people. On my own. I was twenty-two. I was seeing many things I'd never seen before— stenographers and typists and the effect of the war on all these people. I was fascinated, utterly fascinated by it. And so, inevitably, I wanted to write about it. Even more than I wanted to write about what was going on inside me— and plenty was, I can tell you.

BASHFORD & RUZESKY: You have an amazing vocabulary. I was reading Robert Enright's review of *The Hidden Room* and he said there's only one other person who can use "maculate" and that's T.S. Eliot.

PAGE: You know what it means, don't you?

BASHFORD & RUZESKY: No.

PAGE: It means spotted. Dirty. Maculate… immaculate. It has a certain ambiguity. It can mean soiled, I suppose, but it can mean spotted. I used it in "Arras." It's the peacock's tail. But to get back— I don't think my vocabulary's very big, but it may be quirky.

BASHFORD & RUZESKY: Again, in your essay, "Traveller, Journeyman, Conjuror" you talk about being hot or cold when you're writing and I was wondering how you know when you're hot or cold?

PAGE: Do you remember a game in which your friends, while you were out of the room, chose an object in the room which you had to find? You were guided only by their telling you that you were getting hot, or getting cold. It's a feeling of proximity. In the game your friends gave you clues. But when you are writing, some split part of you gives you the clues. It's as if there is a lode that draws you and when you get close to it you know you're hot. It's like a fire. There's some emanation. It doesn't necessarily mean you are writing well, unfortunately!

BASHFORD & RUZESKY: In the film version of one of your short stories you've suddenly become an actor. What was your experience of acting? Did elements of the performing you've done at public readings come into it or was it an entirely different thing?

PAGE: Maybe I should go back a little bit. When I was young I didn't know whether I wanted to act or write. I thought maybe I wanted to act. I had no experience of acting except in school plays and amateur theatre in the Maritimes and I loved it. I simply loved it. But I wasn't very good. It gradually dawned on me that I couldn't play Lady Macbeth and if you're an actor you want to play Lady Macbeth. I realized I hadn't the capacity and maybe I'd better stick to writing. But I fiddled around. I did some radio acting when I was quite young. I had a boyfriend in radio and I wrote a series of duologues that we performed. I've always been interested in theatre. Film has never captured my imagination in quite the way that theatre has.

I put the whole thing completely out of my head. Then thirty years ago Barrie Maclean asked me to play the principal role in a film he wanted to make from one of my stories. I said, "Barrie, you need an actor and I'm not an actor." "No, no," he said, "you don't understand. You'd be right for it. Half of it's camera work." I said, "No, no, no," but anyhow, nothing came of it. Then, when Barrie died suddenly last year, as a memorial to him, I agreed to play in Anna Chernakova's version of the same movie, even though I was too old for the role. I couldn't remember lines. My memory was not as good. So they used voice-over, which I read in a studio, and the only lines I had to say on camera were small bits of dialogue, many of which were spontaneous. I also knew I couldn't act and had no idea what to do in front of the camera. In the theatre you have a certain distance from your audience and if you ham it isn't so noticeable, but if the camera is in your face and you're mugging... There are a lot of uncertainties and unknowns. You never know which part of you the camera is shooting. Are they shooting you entire, or only your left elbow? You don't know. It's a funny feeling. You become almost disembodied. Dismembered is a better way to put it.

Someone had said the less you act on film the better, so most of the time I walked around with no expression on my face at all because I didn't really know what was expected of me. I was given very little direction.

And it's boring! They shoot over and over again. You do the damned thing until you're fed up with it. Much of your spontaneity has gone by the time they're finally satisfied with the camera angle or the lighting. Also, it's collaborative. But I find working with people is always interesting, even as I say it was boring.

BASHFORD & RUZESKY: You wouldn't do it again?

PAGE: No. But once was interesting. I knew film was a great deal of fakery— after all, I had worked at the National Film Board at one time— and I certainly know to what extent it's fakery now. But what really disappointed me was how much of the story was lost in the filming.

BASHFORD & RUZESKY: You're involved in various collaborations. You're working on an oratorio?

PAGE: To celebrate Canadian Composers, Nicholas Goldschmidt dreamed up Music 2000— a Canada-wide festival of music. It began in Whitehorse on the night of the winter solstice and it will move across the country during the year. Lou Applebaum and Mavor Moore have written an opera based on Samuel Butler's *Erewhon* which will be preformed in Victoria. And Derek Holman of Toronto has written an oratorio, "The Hidden Reality," using seven of my poems—one written especially for it. The score calls for the Toronto Symphony Orchestra, the Mendelsson Choir, the Toronto Children's Chorus, and Ben Hepner, if you please! Among the soloists.

BASHFORD & RUZESKY: There are two other collaborations you've been involved in lately. One is the renga you did with Philip Stratford and the other is the exhibition of poems and drawings with Mimmo Paladino in which he took some of your writing and he made drawings from them.

PAGE: The most intimate of all was the renga because my mind was being changed by Philip and Philip's mind was being changed by mine. His mind would be going one direction and mine would jog him off course and vice versa. So it was very intimate. Although impersonal. The correspondence from this period is quite interesting. We used slow mail because he didn't have a fax, and our personal lives never entered into the correspondence at all. He went through a major operation in the middle of it. He never referred to it in any of his letters. There was a very long silence and I thought, "He's bored. This is it." I learned later that he'd been through surgery. But in our letters we began to know each other's minds. That was the closest collaboration. It wouldn't work with everyone. With Paladino there's no collaboration at all, if collaboration means working together. I've never met Paladino. I've never spoken to him. I've never written to him. He's never communicated with me. Francesca Valente, director of the Instituto Italiano di Cultura, Toronto, gave him the poems that she translated into Italian and he came up with his images. It was the least personal collaboration of all. The most abstract, really.

BASHFORD & RUZESKY: But your minds did meet in a distant way.

PAGE: I was in no way indifferent to the way his mind responded but I was not involved. I was interested in seeing what images he drew from my poems but I felt little connection to them. I loved some of the drawings. I'd give anything to own one of them. But they didn't seem to have much to do with me. What he picked from a poem was not the image I would have picked.

BASHFORD & RUZESKY: Your chapbook, *Alphabetical* (Hawthorne Society, 1998), won the 1999 bpNichol Chapbook Award. It seems a change in direction for you. It's playful and also serious. Where did that poem come from?

PAGE: I wrote the word "afterwards" and it seemed to me that afterwards was a very funny word because you couldn't conceive of it if there hadn't been a before. Then I thought, having written a little about afterwards, I'll write a little about "before." And then the whole alphabet seemed to unscroll before me. It amused me to write it and it came easily. And for me it is personal. My background is in it, my family. Bits of it are quite funny, I think.

BASHFORD & RUZESKY: P.K., I get the sense that you're tying up loose ends, which is vaguely disturbing because you're...

PAGE: ...getting ready for departure.

BASHFORD & RUZESKY: What I want to know is what some of those loose ends are.

PAGE: I am preparing for a further journey, there's no doubt about that. I'd like to get my affairs in order. Not to leave a mess for anyone else to deal with. I don't mean that I think I'm going to die tomorrow. I don't. I think I'm going to be here for a while. But there isn't a great deal of time left to do a lot of work in. One seems to be like a magnet in life and one accumulates, whether one wants to or not, an immense amount of matter. And I want to dispose of that. My final whack at controlling things.

Also, I have writing I want to do. I've got all my Mexican and Australian stuff, most of which may be useless except to a biographer. I'd like to get all my papers into some kind of shape. I don't see how one can help but think this way in one's eighties. But it's forward-looking, going with the flow. It's not a closure.

... One book I want to do is the renga with the correspondence with Philip Stratford and an introduction by me and notes within the correspondence to indicate what was happening in Philip's life that slowed the renga down. We called it a renga but of course it isn't. It's just two voices instead of one. I suggested it because a mutual friend told me that Philip was depressed after an operation. I didn't know him all that well, but I thought it might amuse him, prove to be fun. I loved doing it. It was a game.

BASHFORD & RUZESKY: If Arthur [Irwin] were here he'd be sitting in that chair over there and at some point he'd be bound to ask me something like, "Well sir, what do you think about the state of literature in this country?" I want to turn that question on to you.

PAGE: That's just what he'd ask, isn't it? "Is it going anywhere?" I don't know if I'm up to date on the state of literature in Canada. I think we have a large number of very good poets; too many for their own good because they become invisible in the crowd. There's been a burst of a lot of very good poetry. I'm not as up to date on the state of fiction.

Literature will survive. I'm not worried about that. It may be going to fewer and fewer people but it will always survive. It's food.

Excavating Memories

Libby Scheier interviewed by Beverley Daurio

Libby Scheier is the author Saints and Runners: Stories and a Novella, and of four books of poetry: *The Larger Life, Second Nature, SKY— A Poem in Four Pieces*, and *Kaddish for My Father*. Her poetry has appeared in many anthologies, including *Women on War* (Simon & Schuster) and *Poetry by Canadian Women* (Oxford University Press), and her short fiction and criticism have appeared in numerous periodicals and anthologies. She lives in Toronto.

BEVERLEY DAURIO: Some writers seem to keep a gulf of aesthetic distance between their lives and their writing, but you seem to live inside your literary work and to pull your real life through your literary work...

LIBBY SCHEIER: Even before I had theoretical explanations for it, I never did subscribe to the notion that art and therapy are completely separate. My writing always involved aspects of my life, and as far as I can see, it has that function for others as well, even writers who insist on the notion that art is one thing and self-expression is something else, and that using art as therapy cheapens the art. Even if writers are dealing only with the structure of language, they are still dealing with issues that affect their lives.

DAURIO: In "Why Poems Should Not Be Fictions," a poem in *The Larger Life*, you say you write poems partly "because I need an outlet for my polemics/ that is socially acceptable." This indicates a desire for art that critiques society but which will be heard. Would you say this chafing was central to your literary project?

SCHEIER: I don't know what the contradiction is between critiquing society and wanting that to be heard; I think anyone who makes a critique wants it to be heard and wants things to change. I feel a lot of anger and upside-downness about the way things are. A lot of expectations that there are of women in our society have nothing to do with the kind of person I am: they make me feel like I am being put into somebody else's clothes and the clothes don't fit. So, getting heard as to what I am in fact, and not what is required of me in current society, is important to me. Poetry has been a place where I can expose what I know is true, but has not been accepted as true in this society, expose my own experiences which are constantly denied by the mainstream discourse.

DAURIO: One theme that runs through your poetry is the admission of despair, as in "Dry Run," where you allude to the suicides of Anne Sexton and Sylvia Plath; but you immediately counter despair by saying that aggression turned outward is better than aggression turned inward. Do you think this is a realistic possibility for women?

SCHEIER: I don't consider that poem an admission of despair. It's ironic... I like to read it like, oh, gee, all these women committed suicide; let's go for murder. Obviously, I'm not calling for women to commit murder, I'm calling for them not to commit suicide. I'm no doubt speaking to myself as much as anybody else; not to turn the problems inward, against oneself, but to recognize the source of trouble as external and empower yourself to deal with it.

DAURIO: Writing from life makes possible a poem like "Fetal Suite," an examination of pregnancy from many angles: intellectual, emotional, imagistic, and others. How did the opening into such writing happen for you?

SCHEIER: Very spontaneously. At the time of writing *The Larger Life*, I did not have a very formed idea of what my poetic project was. It has become much more formed over the years, though I am still subject to being surprised by what I write. "Fetal Suite" was written when I was pregnant, and for me that was a very bizarre experience, with emotions from feeling wonderful to feeling creepy, as if there were a parasite growing inside me. I just burst into that poem one day, mostly out of that creepy feeling. I had nightmares about giving birth to a snake, and eating my baby— all kinds of cannibalistic and transmutational dreams. And of course, it ends with me being embarrassed, because when the baby is born I immediately fall in love with the baby. When I first read that poem at readings, some people were disgusted, because it was a deconstruction of the usual romanticism around pregnancy. I never had a woman complain about it, because women who had been pregnant recognized the feelings.

DAURIO: You are a feminist, and it's also clear from your poetry and your essays that you are leery of any dogma which might be attached to that label.

SCHEIER: I have always had a lot of struggle and confusion and heartache around the relationship between politics and art and my art. It seems obvious to me, looking back at my last three books, that they are feminist books in the sense that they are written out of women's experience, and I hope in an honest way that gives voice to women's experience in ways that may not have been done. The doors that feminism has opened for me, giving me permission to write my truths, about my pregnancy, about being sexually assaulted when I was a child, have been tremendously liberating, but I do always have this concern of such openings being codified too rigidly. I'm responsible for my own interpretations, and my own writing, so I don't know why I worry about it; certainly, I can do what I want.

DAURIO: In your poems you stay away from traditional form, like sonnets, haiku, or ghazals; rather you stray into a great deal of formal experiment in Second Nature, like "Penises and Vaginas: an essay," which is actually a poem, "My American Heritage," an autobiographical piece, or letters in the form of a poem. Were you purposely pushing at the borders of "poetry," or were these simply natural extensions of require-ments for "saying"?

SCHEIER: I should have subtitled Second Nature "Poems and Prose

Pieces," because there are pieces in there I didn't consider prose *poems*. But there was a sense I had about not wanting to make big distinctions between certain kinds of form, and to show how they inter-relate in my writing process. The weirdest thing I did was to put in a letter that was written by my father. But it was appropriate to what the book was doing; his letter had said it better than I could— it was supposed to be my section in male voice; why not have a real male voice? About form, though: the forms seem to arrive that suit the occasion. Pasteur said, chance favours the prepared mind, and I am interested in the blurring of genres and in formal innovation and experimentation.

DAURIO: There are many poems in *Second Nature* about your son Jacob. How has having a child, a son, affected your poetry and your world view?

SCHEIER: Profoundly. Giving birth was the most ecstatic experience I've ever had. Judy Chicago has discussed the triumphant elements of crowning— that is, when the head emerges from the vagina— and how, if men had it, we'd have been hearing about it over and over again, and isn't it strange that this hasn't found its way into language and artistic expression? Getting pregnant and having and raising a child opened a whole piece of my brain that had been dormant and that I didn't know about. I had an enormous oceanic feeling of warmth when I gave birth, and when I was nursing, that made me feel, not reduced to my biology, but elevated to my biology, glad to be not an individual but part of a universal condition. One of my favourite poems is "For My Son at Age Two." Jacob was going through a period when he wouldn't eat unless we ate from the same plate, and his sense of human community and closeness was something I had forgotten, about what was beautiful about being human. Motherhood has been the most difficult job I've ever had, but also the most satisfying, and it was strengthened by feminism.

DAURIO: SKY is a book-length poem, or, as its title states, *A Poem in Four Pieces*, each of which relates to one of the four elements. Did you write SKY knowing it was going to be a long poem, or did its form evolve during the work on it?

SCHEIER: It evolved. I didn't know it was going to be about the experience of sexual assault in my childhood, either. I didn't know that it would be structured around the four elements. At one point, I found myself describing SKY as a document of healing. But it didn't start that way. The beginnings of the book came out of a discussion I had with Erin Mouré and Gail Scott about how men and women see things. I had raised the cliché of the dark sky at night with all the stars, when you stand and speculate on your place in the universe and how small you are and what is the meaning of it all... I felt then that men and women see that sky in the same way, but Gail and Erin disagreed. So I started writing about the sociology of sky, the sociology of the perceptions of sky, what it means, does it change, the different things it can be, positive and negative, and so on. During the course of writing that, I began group therapy at the Barbara Schlifer Clinic in Toronto, for adult survivors of child sexual abuse and incest. I wrote about that abuse in *Second Nature* in a disguised kind of way, and it worked its way into this sky book I was writing, examining perception and language in relation to a particular image which everybody sees all the time. So there was a kind of excavating for memories going on, and then a kind of excavating around perception and language. SKY is not a book which is a memoir of child sexual abuse; it contains that as part of a whole lot of other explorations.

DAURIO: Do you think that when you knew it was going to be a long poem, that it changed the way you phrased things, the way you wrote?

SCHEIER: Yes, because there are certain things that I do when I write prose fiction: find little problems which I fix structurally, or with more explanation, detail, or description, and in SKY, once the character of the book became clear to me, there were poems which I wrote on purpose, which is not something I do a lot of. "Ocean" and "Fire" were mainly written to flesh out the four-element structure, because they made sense to me, and I had something to say in that imagistic framework. Working on a long poem made me less self-conscious and less worried about each word. I responded, as well, to calls within the language: if I had asked a question earlier in the book, maybe I wanted to echo it somewhere else... It made me very conscious of the way the parts of the book inter-related, and I sometimes re-wrote on that basis.

DAURIO: The first section of SKY, "Sky Narratives," is a rhythmic swing between things that pin one to human reality— like sailboats and children— and emotional and thoughtful meditations about more universal and abstract things... it ends with a poem about the beauties of northern Ontario where there is a kind of synthesis... "our bodies and our minds, our body and our mind." Was this an intentional movement, one of those purposeful constructions?

SCHEIER: The book opens with a consideration of suicide, which is told in the third person, and in fact, it didn't occur to me until the book was quite finished that I was talking about my own feelings. I was coming out of a period of difficulty in my life, as a single parent, alone; also, my child was reaching the age of five, which is how old I was when I was assaulted. All that stuff was coming up in me and I didn't know what to do with it. I was close to the edge before I went into a healing process; I could have gone the other way. SKY is more sober than my other work; I think the irony in my other work helped to distance material I had trouble dealing with. I wasn't conscious of it, but I was dealing with that seduction of the black endlessness of everything, the stasis, and even though that's portrayed as something unpleasant, one is drawn to it, and then back to the kites and the children in the classroom... There are also moments of joy, the sky being like mother, the sky that is tender...

DAURIO: The sky is referred to as mother; so is the ocean, so is the earth... What are you getting at with that?

SCHEIER: I'm getting at mother as the origin, as ocean and earth being the origin, and the ocean inside mother when you are in there as fetus.

Perhaps I was getting at a sense of the primacy of mothers, which has been buried; certainly, when I got to the chant about mother earth, it upset me: the way in which we have crapped on mothers, and the origins of life, and it seems very sad. I would like to see that image of the authority of the mother restored, independently of the image of the father.

DAURIO: The section "Ocean" hints at what is going to come later in the book: "I am frightened of going inside/ again." But it heads off that confrontation with a listing of healthy desires and imagery, like "a blue holy bird in my hair singing," which is like a talisman against danger... as if you are arming yourself and the reader for the coming ordeal in a process of ritual cleansing or purification.

SCHEIER: The line "frightened of going inside again" is an allusion to death, to the sense of death being a return to the fetal state, the ocean. But it also refers to going inside yourself, into memories. The language of "Ocean" is spare; there are short lines, gaps... so there's a kind of chanting quality to it. The blue holy bird is my talismanic image of hope and holiness. I wrote that poem standing on the beach at Long Island, in a safe landscape, the landscape of my childhood, and it felt like a declaration of intention, of what I wanted.

DAURIO: Phyllis Webb has said of SKY that "The central drama is child-rape, but the imaginative range is cosmic." The sexual abuse of the child occurs in the section called "Earth Per Verse," and the recovery of the child's self which is one of the most suspenseful passages I've read in poetry. Was the writing of this cathartic for you or harrowing?

SCHEIER: I was very calm when I wrote it, although it was the culmination of a good deal of harrowing work. I wrote the poem recounting the rape experience first, and I was just relieved that it finally got on paper the way it ought to be, after many many frustrating attempts at writing it that failed. The therapy prepared me to be able excavate down and re-experience the emotions of the time, and because of this I was grateful and relieved and I was satisfied. The other part was written a few months later, and was very directly tied to an experience I had in therapy. I went into a meditation about being in bed as a child, and experiencing a lot of terrifying feelings, and I had an image of a girl with no skin in a black space. I was able to hold it and feel it and so was able to deal with it. Another image came from a pain across my chest, and that is where the image of the little heart came from, the child's heart, which I retrieved. Both of those images were very concrete and visual images: the heart outside my body and the girl with no skin.

DAURIO: The section "Fire" completes the cycle of the elements: there is a lot of anger, burning, explosions. Do you think these things were repressed earlier in the book by the struggle for control before the reclamation of the heart, and that is why they burst out with such force here in the last part of SKY?

SCHEIER: The fire destroys the old ways, but the first poem in this section is about making love, indicating the possibilities of passion after healing. The gist of "Fire" is love: but the word itself doesn't appear there. In order to be ready to destroy everything below, you do have to come to a feeling of strength; in order to destroy what's behind you, you have to have some sense of where you're going, and of your independent existence. Throughout, SKY moves between the individual and the general, and in "Fire," the point of view is coming out of the individual healing and moving back to get the wider view again, and seeing that my trauma is not unique, but part of a large problem, a larger situation, and the solution is large. The last section is not written in a personal syntax; it barely uses the word "I." Someone noted, talking about the "distant amnesia of space" in "Fire," that the ending of SKY calls into question the possibility of getting to memory in any real way; things always return to amnesia. The success I have with my healing will one day be forgotten; the whole business that one is engaged in is very tiny, and one day will be completely gone...

DAURIO: SKY ends, as all your books have, with renewal. Is this a way of saying that we are actually disposed to hope and to the possibilities of life?

SCHEIER: I don't know about "we," but it is saying that I need to end my books this way. I don't tolerate despair very well. I'd rather be alive, and so I need a little hope. Each book also ends with a sense of mystery: respect and admiration for the magic of the universe, not knowing what it's all about. I like the feeling of things being open and unfinished. There is a lot of frustration in trying to figure things out and never quite doing it: a solution is to respect and love the mystery and have hope.

Plurality of Vision

Anne Szumigalski interviewed by John Livingstone Clark

Anne Szumigalski's books of poetry include *Voice, Rapture of the Deep, Dogstones, A Game of Angels,* and *On Glassy Wings.* She has won the Governor General's Award and is also the author of the hybrid texts *The Word, the Text, and the Voice* and *Sermons on Stones.*

JOHN CLARK: The idea of doing a monograph on you is rather daunting. Other people, for example, have said to me, "Where do you begin? How can you hope to come to terms with the complexity of the work; there is so much of it; it is so tightly interwoven with so many images, symbols, facts, etc.— the vision is so expansive. Where can you possibly begin?" Where do you think is a good place to start?

ANNE SZUMIGALSKI: It's very difficult to view one's own work coolly, but I think of myself as having two different personalities in my one self. One of them is very childlike, and I think most people notice that and may be a little impatient about it. And the other one is quite sophisticated and interested in all kinds of conjectures and ideas. Which of those would you like to address first?

CLARK: Well, I suppose in some way the child is of special interest to me because it is where we move, it seems to me, into the whole topic of religious vision or the spiritual perspective. I recall that you have said to me on several occasions that you see yourself as primarily a *religious* poet; or, if I can refer back to a remark you made, "Ed Dyck says I am essentially a religious poet and he is right."

SZUMIGALSKI: That's quite true, but I think he also added that it was in a very unconventional way. I'm not, of course, particularly attached to any one religion, but I think I view the world in that spirit. That's the way I look at the whole world. I believe, with Blake, that the body is simply an emanation of the spirit, so that the spirit comes first and will remain afterwards, even if that spirit remains in the form of some printed work. Does that make any difference, in what form it is? Is that another body?

CLARK: I recall you using that quotation often, "the body is the emanation of the soul," and it reminds me very much of current thinkers who talk about *panentheism*, the notion that an absolute or some sense of God is completely incarnate in creation. It is an attempt to get beyond the old Christian dichotomy of creator and creation, in which creation really brings up the rear very much, ushering in a new spirit of openness to the phenomenal world, seeing the sacred as fully incarnate or imbued in creation. And I get a strong sense of that incarnational theology... or— I don't want to use the word theology because I know you're a poet, not a theologian... but that incarnational spirituality in your work.

SZUMIGALSKI: Yes, well, I suppose I would like to say something about that. I agree with some Jewish thinkers whose view is that without man there is no God, because God rests in man and so on... and here I am a Blakean again. I want to say that we have imagined a God with enough imagination to imagine us with enough imagination to imagine God (Him, Her, or It). I like to think of God in the sense of the *pleroma*, that's the fullness, the light, a perfect beginning and end. But if I didn't think of it like that, then, it would be unknown to me, and if we all didn't think about it, then it would be unknown to all of us. I don't think there is an absolute anything, or anything is absolute, which ever way you want to look at that.

CLARK: So there is a strong intuitive sense of the pleroma as fullness of being or holiness of being, without falling prey to any kind of doctrinal commitment or the counting of angels on heads of pins, etc.

SZUMIGALSKI: Well, I think all those things extremely interesting, and I don't think of those as falling prey to something. I think those are ways of looking at it. I think I'm one of those people who likes to stand back and look at it, perhaps, from more distance, but I don't think any of those things are not true. I think one of the big problems we— or Western thought, has— is taking it for granted that two different things are necessarily untrue to each other. There is no reason why twenty-five different views of the universe shouldn't all be the right view. They probably are. I think now that we have physicists with open minds who can look at these things, that this idea of *plurality* is really important.

The same beam of light may go through more than one aperture at the same time. That tells us something about truth; I think that just because one thing is true, it doesn't make anything else false.

CLARK: So the only problem would be in attempting to assert the authority of one aperture over others.

SZUMIGALSKI: Yes... but I think what one does is probably choose one's own little aperture to go through, because if you don't do that, then your thought becomes disseminated; it melts away... it is very difficult to think of something unless you have a path to think along, I'm saying, or an aperture to go through with your beam of light. So that, in fact, the choice is very important to the person who makes it, but let's say that I don't think the pleroma cares two hoots which one you choose. I don't know if that makes any sense to you...

CLARK: It certainly seems to me that the plurality or the pluralism that you are talking about is evident in your work, and it is very evident in the breadth of your reading where you are quite knowledgeable in the areas of life sciences, mathematics and modern physics, particularly in the new physics with all its mystical overtones, and in history and various cultures, and of course, obviously, in modern literature. It seems to me that the advantage poets or creative artists always have is that they can take that plurality of vision and wed it to something which is quite integrated. And that's where, in some ways, the artist has a supreme advantage over the theologian or the philosopher. The artist does not have to come up with a balanced proposition. He or she doesn't have to stick to the Aristotelian ground rules. He or she can go beyond the premises of simple formal logic and arrive at much higher levels of synthesis, and that's what I see going on in your work. So, I delight in the plurality, on one hand, while on the other I appreciate the fact that it is grounded in some kind of intuitive field which you call the imagination. Does that make any sense?

SZUMIGALSKI: Yes... in the imagination, of course. I keep on saying, you know, if I have to choose somebody to follow, I think it will be Blake; though I don't always keep to what Blake says to me, any more than anyone should keep to what their Master or Mistress is telling them to do. But... ah, yes, I think of things in that direction very much. I was going to now take, as an example, visual art, where you see many "have been and are and will be" theories on visual art. But great works of art, no matter which theory they think they're following, always transcend those theories, and you can see that in sculpture very often. Yes, of course, this is the way to sculpt, perhaps, the human figure: but some things turn out to be plaster Madonnas and some turn out to be Michaelangelo's "David." So, what are we going to do about that... that is the ground thing. And I think that's the same with literary art, or any way of looking at things, for me, anyway.

CLARK: So, the imagination is capable of producing works of art that reflect, or contain within them, a gnosis (if you will), that is far beyond our intellectual and theoretical attempts to catch up with it.

SZUMIGALSKI: Yes, but I think we all feel like that, really, because we don't cancel out all the great art works of history because we have a new theory of art. We don't do that. If we did, we'd be even more foolish than we already are... a new idea in literature, a new idea in visual art or music, that doesn't cancel out the old ideas. In fact, they'll keep on coming back; it's just the way we look at things at a particular moment. And I think I'd rather use the word *moment* than *time*, as I find the concepts of time quite difficult to express, though I have my own ideas about them. The other day, while I was going through the works of my childhood, I found a whole exercise book in which I had done twenty-two different diagrams of what I thought time was. And when I looked at them I realized, in spite of the smudgy pencil and the strange remarks I had written underneath, I am still in that exercise book, still making these diagrams and still hoping that one of them will lead me on to something else. I don't want to stop here any more than anyone else does. I want to go on to other ideas so that when I'm talking about my ideas, come tomorrow I might have changed my mind about some of them. Luckily, because I don't think anybody's mind should stand still on one thing. Though there are, in the end, things or foundations, bricks, stones, prairies, on which one builds houses which are ideas, which are *the* idea, sometimes.

CLARK: Do your meditations on time have anything to do with the fact that the intuition or the vision of eternity crops up so much in your work, and usually implicitly rather than explicitly, with all kinds of angels, seraphim and what-have-you? But always pointing towards an opening into eternity.

SZUMIGALSKI: Well, that is my way of looking at time; but what I suppose I'm saying is that I have a very firm (let's say philosophical) idea of what I think time is and I'm looking at this thing, but the little telescopes which I am arranging or making for myself are every day different ones, through which I am looking at my same time, my same idea of eternity. So tomorrow I may construct another telescope, but the foundations of my ideas about eternity haven't changed so much as my view of those foundations.

CLARK: So you are again making a distinction between some kind of almost unconsciously engendered intuition and a more intellectual or theoretical grasp of what's actually going on.

SZUMIGALSKI: Yes, and that does bring us to another point and that is that when writing poetry, one of the balances that has to come is a balance between imagination and the intellect. Some poetry doesn't seem to care much for the intellect. I don't think that's the way I can go. I think that some poetry is very intellectual but doesn't seem to have the spark of the imagination. For me, it's very important to follow both these things. Maybe through two different apertures. Maybe they are both light.

CLARK: And somehow in the poem they achieve a kind of gestalt.

SZUMIGALSKI: Well, this kind of synthesis is probably what I'm trying for, but when I'm speaking like this it sounds as though I believed that I can arrange my head to write a poem. I can't do that. There is more than one space in my head and there are spaces which are not under the foot of my will, let's say. (That's a very contortionist way of looking at things. Perhaps I can draw a drawing of this contortion with a foot on the will or the head.) But, all the same, there are things which people may call inspiration or given things, but which I consider as things that parts of my mind are using, and that when I open my mouth, the result of those thoughts will come out. But I don't have any obvious will over that; it seems to have a will of its own, which sounds, perhaps, a bit too wafty for what I mean.

CLARK: It certainly made me think immediately of Jung's theories of personality *types*, the various functions of the psyche, etc.: the rational, the emotional, the intuitive, the sensory; and you drag in theories of the unconscious, individuation and what-have-you, and certainly a reading of Jung has given me some insight into the complexity of your world... and I don't know whether you've actually bothered reading all that much Jung. I think you've come to this vision of yourself quite naturally.

SZUMIGALSKI: Yes, that's quite true; it is certainly true that I would have had this vision of myself anyway. But, of course, since I've thought this through, I have indeed read Jung and I agree, of course. It's wonderful, when you do this kind of thing, to suddenly realize that this is something that somebody else or lots of other people agree with and understand, but there are always differences in the way. We cannot entirely agree with any philosopher or any idea because we are, after all, separate beings: in spite of Jung's thinking that perhaps, in a lot of ways, we are not. I think there are so many mysteries there that it is very difficult to tread through them, and that everybody who does tread through them will think of themselves as having taken a different path. But that doesn't matter, as I've said before. The idea of the collective unconscious is obviously one which one is born with, that idea. Perhaps as babies we know these things. Later on we unlearn them, but when we meet them again in a book or in conversation, then we recognize them. There are too many things to explain, especially in the literary world, to throw these ideas out. But is it, as I think E.F. Dyck says, that it has something to do with the energy produced by thought. Now this may appear to be a little romantic, and I was surprised to hear this particular person speak in this way; for a mathematician, it seemed to me to be excitingly imaginative... however, I sort of grew up reading about books. In fact, I grew up in a family that liked to read not only books, but a great many reviews and criticisms of books, so I'm always completely surprised that the thinkers of this world, and even inventors whose thinking is perhaps more practical, seem to come out with the same things at the same time. There has only got to be one book, perhaps, on an obscure thing, say about the struggles of Toussaint L'Ouverture or somebody like that, then somehow five books come out with this same theme, and none of these people knew that others were writing these things. They just came to it by themselves. I find these things very difficult to explain. Perhaps Dyck is right and it has something to do with the energy produced by all this thinking. And there are quite a few people who think, of course.

CLARK: Just for the record, why did Toussaint L'Ouverture's name just come to mind?

SZUMIGALSKI: Toussaint L'Ouverture was the person who originally freed Haiti from white rule and he was the first black president. It's a lovely name, which to me means "All Saints of the Opening." I just thought of him as we've been thinking about Haiti lately, and he's one of the people whom I was surprised to learn had five different writers working independently on him in different parts of the world. This happens so often on other topics. Don't you find that yourself?

CLARK: Yes. I don't want to drag any more labels in, but it certainly makes me think of Jung's theory of synchronicity. One of the things I appreciate about your work, incidentally, is the way in which these marvellous visionary qualities and energies crop up effortlessly. So one gets the sense that there is never any intellectual pushing going on. That the intellect does its job, that the imagination does its job, and out of it, on some quite unconscious level, things are put together that grow. I guess to come around to your work, for example, one of the really dominant images in your poetry is that of vegetative, organic growth. There are always things growing, plants, etc... like the tree in the poem "Quince."

SZUMIGALSKI: Yes, I am interested in plants and I am frequently rather disappointed that most people seem to go with the idea that plants are not living. On the other hand, animals are living, so it is wrong to kill them. But what about plants? The idea that plants have no consciousness at all doesn't seem to fit what I see. I've only to look at a flowering crabapple tree to know that. Don't tell me that tree doesn't know that it's flowering. Because we are so distant now in our physical beings from plants, we can't understand how they do this. We imagine that all creatures must, in fact, do it through the same channels as ourselves. So I think the vegetative kingdom is what lies beneath everything and, of course, physically it does. It is the foundation of the biosphere, it is what comes first; at the bottom of the food chain we always find plants.

CLARK: Somewhere, in the dark recesses of the limbic mind, we are, perhaps, plants?

SZUMIGALSKI: Well, I think that we are. I think people know that we are. There are parts of us which contain plants and without those plants we would not be as we are. I think most people, running from job to television to job, don't realize that plants are the foundation of our life. And I think more distress in this world is caused by cruelty to plants, in fact, than cruelty to animals. Just think of what's happening to the earth when we cut down all those trees. That is definitely cruelty to plants, wouldn't you say?

CLARK: Definitely. But if I could digress a little, your earlier reference to Blake has had a much quoted phrase of his rolling around in the back of my mind for the last few minutes and, again, it is the notion of seeing the infinite in a grain of sand. It seems to me that not only do you see it in a grain of sand, you see the infinite in the entire cosmos and that the breadth of your vision is really quite astonishing. I think also of that statement you've often made with reference to your love of Saskatchewan, your love of the prairie, and how you are essentially, foundationally, a prairie writer, but that you don't "write into the prairie," you "write out of it." I think it's a remark that has caused more than a few people to stop and reflect, and perhaps you could enlarge on that.

SZUMIGALSKI: Yes, I'd like to talk about that because, on the face of it, a lot of my poems are about childhood and various places. I've lived in a lot of places and a lot of my poems are about these places. But on the other hand, the whole of my work is so much influenced by the prairie that even these would not exist, these poems would not exist, unless I lived in this particular place. I know that if I had stayed in my native land or lived in Europe (as I, of course, have sometimes), I wouldn't be able to write the poems that I'm writing now. It wouldn't have turned out like this. I would have written poetry, I would have always written something, but this breadth, this allowance of breadth and space, I would not have had that. Somehow the prairies have given me a sort of license, it's as though it were in fact a license, a piece of paper on which is written, "Think as widely as you want to, infinite is the space up and down. Jump into it. Don't confine yourself." And I know that's what I have felt on the prairie, and I know it's the foundation of all my poetry. But I think people find it really difficult to accept that, because, of course, sometimes I write poems about Britain. I write poems about Wales, I write poems about England, Poland, the low countries, many places in which I've been, and those places are important in the poems; but the wider vision, the foundation of my idea of space and place is the prairies, where I have lived such a long time, much more than half my life. Perhaps people will find that difficult.

CLARK: I think difficult only in the sense that to think through that process of writing out of the prairie, you actually have to move out of an empirical mode and into a kind of mystical or metaphysical or surreal mode. I think, also, to go back to your earlier mention of the visual arts, that literature in this country has, at least in English, a tendency to, again, work alongside the Group of Seven and Robert Bateman and Alex Colville. I don't know if the literature has produced too many Magrittes or Chagalls, and I think I tend to think of you as... visually, in the company of Magritte, Chagall or Rousseau. How do you locate yourself, in terms of writing, in English literature in Canada these days?

SZUMIGALSKI: You mean in terms of where I think I am vis à vis the English speaking literature or Canadian things?

CLARK: Yes, specifically Canadian writing.

SZUMIGALSKI: Well, I think I am odd-woman-out in Canadian writing. There are, of course, a few people who mind about the things that I mind and write about them, but there are not that many. Canadian literature tends to be much more interested in narrative— I'm speaking of poems— than I tend to be. I think of my poems as being suspended in time, so that time doesn't necessarily pass between the first stanza and the last. That's very unusual for Canadian literature. But we do what we must... I must write like this. I can't change myself into somebody else and that doesn't mean that I don't enjoy a lot of different kinds of literature.

But I am glad now that I see many more imaginative writers

coming up in Canada, because I think that's one of the things we have lacked. Does that mean that Canadians have not been imaginative? I don't think so. I think Canadian people altogether, and particularly in the arts, have not thought of themselves as being imaginative. Somehow it's been hidden like a light under a bushel basket. I've often wondered about that. Why didn't it burn the basket? It must have been an oil lamp, mustn't it?

CLARK: It leads me to wonder about the imagination in Canadian writing and the fact that we're still a relatively youthful country and, in many ways, we're not very far from the frontier. A British academic I knew at UBC said to me, many years ago, that when he first moved to Vancouver he was absolutely astounded one day when a military plane went down behind North Vancouver, and when they finally found the wreckage, after searching in vain for weeks, it was only about a hundred yards from a major highway. The crash site, in fact, was not very far outside the city, and he was overwhelmed by the density of the bush and the fact that the wilderness is still right there on your doorstep in most of Canada. And I think as a result of that, and because so many people work in resource-based industries and what-have-you, that we're still very, very close to the frontier, so perhaps there is a kind of literature that goes along with that. And it has to be narrative in a very empirical and historically pertinent way. And maybe, when you think of the imaginative work that is going on in Europe and Latin America, and oddly enough, less so, I would think, in the English tradition than on the continent, perhaps there is some sense of antiquity that you need before you can push off confidently into the imagination.

SZUMIGALSKI: Well, I think that is a possibility, and I certainly think that a lot of Canadians writing in English have thought themselves part of the British tradition. And lately, perhaps, as more a part of the American tradition. But speaking of the wilderness, isn't it into the wilderness that we go when we want to meet God? Don't we find there burning bushes, don't we find clouds on top of mountains out of which the voice of God speaks? The wilderness is extremely important to me. One of my memories of first coming to Canada and seeing a map of Saskatchewan was that to the south, to the north and also to the west, there were areas on which the word "wilderness" was printed. I found that extremely exciting, and it was my desire immediately to get into that wilderness and see what was to be seen there, hoping, I suppose, for a burning bush. One day, I was in the south of the province, where we lived for a while on the edge of the Big Muddy Wilderness, a place where wilderness was called wilderness. I was walking along on the stony and dry plain when, looking up, I saw a cloud, a small cloud in a cloudless sky. It moved across the sky and it came, more or less, over where I was, and I was looking at it when suddenly a bolt of lightning came out of the cloud and hit the ground (probably several miles away), and I thought to myself, it is very surprising that I can't see the hand of God throwing down this bolt of lightning. That was the only thing that surprised me about this encounter. So I believe that it is taking the imagination into the wilderness that is very important. That is where things come together. We can't always be in the midst of people; we have to go into the wilds, and it's there that we have mystical experiences of being one with the biosphere, first, and then, of course, with all creation. I think that's the place where I learned most of the foundations of my writing in Canada. I don't know; I do like the wilderness a great deal, but of course my wilderness in this part of Canada is an open, stony wilderness, while what you're talking about is the wilderness that consists of heavy forest. Is there any difference between these things? I don't know. Would I have been so inspired if I had gone to B.C. and seen that kind of wildness? I suppose I would have got used to it. I sometimes try to think my way into these things. When I'm in the mountains or forests, while I may feel a little strange, I think, "But if I had come here to live, how would I have arranged my thoughts to accept this different kind of landscape?"

CLARK: The poet, George McWhirter, has talked about coming to Canada from Ireland, with nary a tree in Ireland, and coming through

Spain and Mexico and finally arriving on the west coast, and saying something to the effect that even now the landscape totally dominates on the west coast, but it pushes you in a particular direction. I don't think it opens you "out" to some sense of the infinite, as you say the prairie does. On the west coast, he would say, it seems to push you into the minutiae of the world around you, the rocks and pebbles on the beach, the drift wood, and because it is overcast much of the time, you have a low cloud cover overhead that, again, pushes you down into the things of the earth and the density of the forests. But, I suppose, in both cases, if you don't dress for the weather, the wilderness can kill you.

SZUMIGALSKI: Well, I think one of the excitements of being in the wild places is the fact that it can kill you. I know that if it were to get colder on the prairies, for instance, supposing five degrees colder, that would make our summer so short that we couldn't grow anything. We couldn't grow any crops and, perhaps, if that happened, we would have to abandon the prairies as a place where we could live all year round. And if you go out on the prairie in the middle of winter, and you don't have any kind of support, you probably will die. And if you go out on the prairies in the middle of summer, where there is no shade, you will probably die. I think that the feeling that the natural world is not going to particularly care for you because you are human is a very exciting one.

CLARK: Certainly the fact of the wilderness on your doorstep makes you profoundly aware of the contingency of your own life and the life of the species, which is one of those, I think, central intuitions that we have somehow lost in the modern world, the idea of the contingency of human beings on each other for simple survival. And it's our amnesia about the reality of contingency that sort of leads us into the hubris of so much modern thought— the ridiculous heresy that we're pulling our own strings, for example, that kind of ego-based reasoning.

SZUMIGALSKI: Yes, that we know what's best for everything.

CLARK: Exactly.

SZUMIGALSKI: We apparently don't know any of that.

CLARK: When you were talking about the cloud and the bolt of lightning, I was trying to recall a phrase or a definition for mythology that a German theologian had given once, and it was something to the effect that in mythic thinking the phenomenal world, the material world, or nature if you will, is simply the overt working of some invisible force and that seems to be fairly common to most notions of mythic thinking, that is, it functions as a kind of metaphor for the ineffable. How do you relate to the idea of mythology? Would you see a lot of your poetry as being a kind of myth-making?

SZUMIGALSKI: I don't think of it as that when I'm writing, but a lot of other people have, I'm not sure I should say "accused" me of that, or expressed that feeling. But I do see what I write about as being concerned, essentially, with underlying myths. I think most writers are like that; we are relating all the time not only to the myths that have been brought forward by our forebears, but all writers are, in a way, making myths. Though, I think there is a distinction between mythic thinking and actual myth-making. Because myths, as we all know, do tend to be narratives or stories about mythic people. But mythic thinking, that is something slightly different, and I think I would certainly go with what you say there. A mythic idea of the universe, for instance, where myth is a story that is true but not fact. Where my work is concerned, I might add, perhaps it is syntax that ties my language to my theology or mythology. But it's definitely the rhythm and sound of language that ties it to my religious feelings. The chant of the rhyme, the song of the breath of the vowels, the mystery created by the magician's word, by the spell of repeated sounds, endless, endless sound, beat and cadence carrying the desire of the spirit to reach Oneness— the true universe. If it means anything, I think the same thing of drumming or dancing. Rain on the roof, the crashing of lake ice at freeze-up or break-up.

CLARK: Just to refine the distinction a little more, Anne, and in response to your sense of myth as truth not fact, I was just recalling the way Eliade, for example, talks about the true myth as being that kind of sacred narrative that takes the initiate, the believer, back in some way to an experience of origins, of that sense of the numinous at creation. And I find a lot of that in your work. But the interesting thing is that you do two things: you tend to take the reader back to that sense of the freshness of existence, back to that sense of the first day of the dawning of creation; but you also don't simply recapitulate old paradigms. There is always something absolutely new in the way that you'll set up some of your pieces. And I'm thinking particularly of some of the pieces in *Rapture of the Deep*, for example, like that lovely tale about the nuns living high up on the cliffsides, lowering baskets to the people below and what-have-you. So there is this marvellous mythic quality to your work and yet, at the same time, there is absolutely nothing remotely conventional about them.

SZUMIGALSKI: Well, of course, it is something that happened. I often do begin with something that really happened, and it really happened that during the Dark Ages both monks and nuns, in the fastnesses of their Irish and Welsh caves by the sea and rocks, did in fact keep learning alive. And the way they got the people to follow after them was by asking those people who were feeding them for some children to bring up or raise, so that there would be more monks and nuns to keep this learning alive. And so works of mine like this begin with very simple historical facts. But from these historical facts, I think of them as mythic because they become truths, and I think perhaps that's not quite so much a myth, it's not so much a legend, it's a different world. Every time I write a poem, I think of myself going into a world which is a great deal more real than the world in which I sit down in my kitchen and talk to John about my peculiar ideas. It is the real world, and each of these worlds is a different world. I know, if you've noticed, I don't write about the same world in two poems; I go into another world in which other things have happened. So these are all worlds. They are rather like dreams in that way; they aren't dreams, of course, but in the way that we often go into our dreams, we go into another world that we haven't been into in any other dream. That's what I'm speaking about. When you're talking about creation, I think that, for me, it is important to create this world; but when I'm doing it, I don't think of myself as having created it, so much as going into it, and deciding to live in this particular world of this poem until the poem is finished. And there are many thousands of such worlds. And I wonder, do you go into those things when you are writing poems, or is that just something I particularly do?

CLARK: Well, I suppose that's where one could get into the metaphysics of the thing. I know that you have read quite widely in mystical theology, and you're certainly familiar with a lot of mystical writings, particularly the well-known women mystics of medieval times. And I would guess that when you're working within a mystical tradition that there is always the sense of moving out of the world of illusion, or Maya, or whatever one would call it, and moving into, ultimately, closer and closer, to some kind of final revelation of the Real, as they refer to it in Islamic thought, or Nirvana, or whatever. So the mystical traditions usually, I would think, move towards some sense of disclosure of a final reality. But the interesting thing in your work is that, and in that way it is really quite open to the twentieth century, I think we've passed beyond the point where one can finally submit to the authority of any one tradition, so that the beauty of your work is that it does take you a very long way, as you say, into new worlds, without demanding that at the end of it you make some final submission to Yahweh or whatever.

SZUMIGALSKI: No, that's quite true, because these worlds have, or are worlds with, different Gods, perhaps, and I am only speaking in a rather light way about those people who live in those worlds; they have different views on the eternal. I don't like to think of myself as having created these worlds, as I have said, I'm just going into them, stepping into these various, strange (to some people) but very familiar to me— these worlds are more familiar to me than my own familiar world, which you may think of as everyday. I think this (everyday world) is more strange for me than those worlds. So that however peculiar the things my people do in their world, they are not so strange to me as things that people do in this world in which we are speaking.

CLARK: No, and I think it's only, again, the language of anthropologists or sociologists that refer to this as *ordinary* or consensual reality, and that just points at this kind of mediating reality that we share in common with others, as a way of going about the business of everyday things. But you are quite right, the everyday does seem remarkably strange to anyone who spends time in the imagination. I guess, in some way, what I would like to talk a little bit about at this point is, if we can talk at all about influences, that is the kinds of poets, thinkers and what-have-you that have played some part in the development of your own poetic voice. Blake certainly has come up before in this respect.

SZUMIGALSKI: Well, I think I would probably put Blake first because I have been reading Blake, or listening, before I could read, to Blake for so many years that I'm sort of definitely Blake imbued. But I think other influences are not necessarily poetic influences. I think I've probably very much been influenced by visual artists whom I admire very much, and other parts of life as well.

I'm *very* interested in the natural sciences. So who is the influence to me? I mean if I had to say, as I once was asked, I think, to say to the library which books had influenced me. I thought very seriously about them and one of the ones that I cited was *Bud's Flora* because— I didn't only mean that book, I meant *Florae* or *Floras*, for those books about plants have influenced my whole life. That's not necessarily a poetic or literary influence, but it is a great influence in my life and I think that to be curious about all these things gives you— gives me, particularly, many of the things that I need for poems. I must know these things, I must know about animals, about their physical world. I must know that, and I read a lot about that all the time. I don't just sit down and read poetry all the time. So it would be very difficult for me to, say, pick out six names and say I've been influenced by these people, except possibly Blake— and some mystical writers. You're quite right about that. But like most people who've spent a childhood in Anglican Britain, the greatest influence, of course, is reading the Bible all the time.

CLARK: The King James version?

SZUMIGALSKI: The King James version, yes, and surprisingly, the *Book of Common Prayer*. Why is it such an influence? It influences your whole idea about language, that's why, the whole idea about the particular language you are using. I can give you some other people who have influenced me, but you might be surprised by them... one of my great influences, I think, is Camus, the novelist. I was reading him early, of course; part of his life was contemporary with mine, so I read him because he was there and he was writing. But since then, since all this length of time, I keep reading his work and I keep being more and more influenced by him. Surprisingly I'm not, I think, at all influenced by Jean-Paul Sartre, who also is a contemporary and fellow existentialist, but I am very much influenced by Camus.

CLARK: There is a sense I have of England through writers, and there is a quality of you and your work that very much reminds me of that particular world of England. And yet it is transposed to the prairies and, as you say, opened up in all kinds of remarkable ways here, and it's that meeting of those two worlds that makes you quite unique, I think, in Canadian writing.

SZUMIGALSKI: Well, you may be surprised to hear that by the age of ten I had decided that I couldn't possibly live in Britain and had to move somewhere else. I felt even then very much hemmed in and stultified by it, but I thought probably what I could do was live in Europe somewhere. I had not thought of coming to North America. That had not been one of my thoughts as a child. And so... I was really pushing against that. I think all those conventions which one should sort of imbibe, didn't take on me at all. I was continually getting into trouble for not knowing what I ought to have known or done, without being told. I could never deal with that kind of thing at all and of course, when thinking of my home as being typically middle class, it wasn't really. We probably had less money than most middle-class families, a large family, and also my mother was a very eccentric person... my father would take us to church while my mother... belonged possibly to the old religion, and she was a person who took us out on midsummer night to dance in the woods and told us all sorts of other things... and she read a lot to us, so I don't think that's typical at all. I don't know why I felt I had to leave my native place, but I think a lot of people are like that. I think there are people who find their place at home where they were born, and there are people who will look for another place, and some of us are lucky enough to find the place we were looking for. We're just lucky.

CLARK: And you had that sense upon arrival in Saskatchewan?

SZUMIGALSKI: Well, the first year I was in Saskatchewan I had a very difficult time getting used to the prairie, because I wasn't used to these wide spaces, except on the sea, and I think the wide open spaces of the prairie caused a peculiar psychological disorder, which was a fear of knives. Did you know about that?

CLARK: No.

SZUMIGALSKI: I haven't written about that, yet, but I'm going to think about that... well, I found out many years later what was wrong. I had, at the time, two very small children and at night I wouldn't go to bed unless I had locked up all the knives and hidden the key. Of course, I didn't know why I was doing this, but I found out afterwards that it's quite common. A disturbed young mother will do that because she doesn't feel quite safe where she is, so she fears she may sleep walk and kill her children, and that's why she does it. But, of course, thank goodness I didn't know that at the time; if I had, I would have been a lot more frightened than I was actually. So after about six months or a year, it wore off, and I think it's just the sort of, maybe it's the trauma of the war years and completely changing one's life and not knowing where things are going that brings these things on... I think that's the only sort of terror that I've had so far... just that one.

CLARK: In mentioning the difficulty of those early years, it just dawned on me that in many ways your early life was the kind of life... completely different kinds of books would be written about. Swept off your feet by an army man and then off to Wales to do a bit of farming, then both of you just sort of wash your hands of the whole European world. At which point you come almost directly to Saskatchewan?

SZUMIGALSKI: Yes.

CLARK: It sort of seems to me that there are any number of different books from all of this; certainly the last move throws you into Martha Ostenso country. And yet, you don't produce any of those books. You don't produce epics of war. You don't produce epics regarding emigration... you do something which is entirely different, and I would suppose that one would have to do a lot of digging in your work to see subtle references to any of that background.

SZUMIGALSKI: Well, I think I do write about these things, quite occasionally. I think the book with Terry Heath has quite a lot of poems about the war in it.

CLARK: But when you write about the war, from what I have seen of a few war poems, it is on a very general level, with lots of symbolism and figurative language, but not so much the first person— this is what it was like when I landed with the troops in Normandy.

SZUMIGALSKI: No, I haven't written about those things, and people always ask me to do it, but one must go with one's imagination.

CLARK: Exactly. I guess the point I'm getting around to is that somehow the imagination is so powerful and so volitional on its own, that it allows very little of the autobiographical into the work explicitly.

SZUMIGALSKI: That's probably quite true. I think something more fundamental interests me. I mean, something that belongs to everybody.

CLARK: Which again puts you very much at odds with, as you say, the bulk of the writing done, which is very much concerned with personal narrative, or very concerned with social justice in a sort of historical sense. But not coming at the realities of pain and suffering and ecstasy, from the direction that you're coming.

SZUMIGALSKI: I think a lot of my works are about justice, but it's not social justice. It's the justice of the universe. The balance of things... in the inevitable balance of things. Which is justice to me.

CLARK: Many people really do seem to have a hard time getting at the complexity and density of your poetic line, and the larger shape of the work in general. And you work so much in terms of juxtaposition and the effects created by these alignments of different things... as well as the enormous range of the music in your language, and sometimes the music far outweighs the syntax or the sense of the thing. It's, as I say, a very sophisticated langauge, and I'm wondering if there have been writers along the way who have contributed, to some degree, to the sophistication of your poetic line...

SZUMIGALSKI: Well, I do read a lot of European poets... that's quite true and, as a young woman, I carried Baudelaire's *Les Fleurs du mal* with me all over Europe. But one hesitates to sort of name three or four of them, because there are so many when I'm reading. And, of course, there are even British poets who have influenced me a lot. I find that many of these influences are sort of immediate, but I'm not sure whether they are influences. For instance, if I find myself in a mood in which I don't believe I'm ever going to write a poem again, and you yourself know that this happens quite frequently to poets, I immediately get out a few books of poetry and I read those books and, if I like these people's work a lot, I immediately begin to write poetry. Now, that isn't to say that my poetry is a bit like theirs. A lot of people whose poetry I admire very much don't write like me at all. But the *idea* of the possibility of getting through all this stuff to write one's best poetry, that's what I'm looking for.

Lost Presence

Fred Wah interviewed by Lola Lemire Tostevin

Fred Wah is the author of sixteen volumes of poetry and prose poetry, including *Waiting for Saskatchewan, Music at the Heart of Thinking,* and *Alley Alley Home Free,* and the prose work *Diamond Grill.* He teaches English at the University of Calgary.

LOLA LEMIRE TOSTEVIN: You were born in Swift Current, Saskatchewan, and lived there until you were four years old. In your book *Waiting for Saskatchewan,* you write that you want it back, that you are waiting for Saskatchewan to appear again over the edge. Does this indicate a nostalgia for the past, for lost presence? Do you believe that through writing you can retrieve that absence?

FRED WAH: The term nostalgia bothers me. What that is, in the first poem of the book, is trying to deal with a geographical reality or concreteness that we all carry. Place as stain, the stain the world makes on a person or vice versa. Although we went back to Saskatchewan on visits, I didn't grow up there and there's something unresolved about that place for me. I live in the mountains now, and this might be one reason for it: the memory, or if you want, the nostalgia, of the flat, the plain. But I think it's something more specific in my life that I was never able to deal with, never able to fully imagine. Since I left at such a young age, the images aren't totally clear. In that sense I feel it still owes me. The place still owes me. I felt that in order for my body to become a complete body in the world I had to have this kind of accounting.

TOSTEVIN: So you're using writing to retrieve those images from the past.

WAH: Yeah, I guess. I don't know if that's the purpose of the writing. Certainly in the act of writing, that's one of the things I'm doing.

Conjuring up the images, the memories, the residue. There's a residue from the past that I've never dealt with so the writing is helping to do that, but I don't know that writing is the only way of doing that.

TOSTEVIN: Writing takes place in the present. How can you retrieve something from the past through the present act of writing?

WAH: Except that language is a stream that comes out of the past and carries with it the weight of time and space. I trust that language carries with it information, not necessarily about anything other than itself, and that it's all there, and that fascinates me. It fascinates me that language can reveal to us somehow any of that.

TOSTEVIN: There's been a great deal of emphasis placed by women on restoring the mother, or the pre-Oedipal psychical stage of development. Many women writers have tried to displace the authority of the father and restore the influence of their mothers. You seem to be preoccupied in finding the father in *Waiting for Saskatchewan*. There's more emphasis on the Oriental side through your father than the Swedish side through your mother. Do the images that you are trying to clarify reside in the tracing back to the male parent? Does it reside in the name of the father? Why not through the mother and the Swedish roots?

WAH: Okay. This is difficult. I've thought about this and I really don't know except I suspect there are several reasons, the main one being that my father died and my mother is still alive. He died when he was quite young and a lot of what I'm dealing with is his death, his absence, the fact that I didn't have part of my life to share with him, although we didn't necessarily share a lot when he was alive. We didn't have that close a relationship although I greatly admired him. Another thing I suppose is that I'm male. Also the Chinese, the exotic aspect of that fascinates me.

TOSTEVIN: Why would the Chinese element be more exotic than the Swedish?

WAH: More exotic because it's more mysterious. The story around my grandfather and father is more mysterious than the story around my mother and her parents from Sweden. That's a fairly clear story— Europeans move to Canada, etc. But my Chinese grandfather atypically married an English woman. Also when I was a kid in elementary school, we had to fill out these forms on registration day and one of the things we had to put down was our racial origin and the teacher told me to put down "Chinese." We weren't allowed then to put down "Canadian." That wasn't considered a racial origin. It's illegal now to ask for anyone's racial origin in Canada, but at that time you wrote down where your father came from. It had nothing to do with the mother. But as you know in *Waiting for Saskatchewan*, the last section of the book is called "Father/Mother Haibun." I intentionally tried to engage some of the mother stuff partly as a way of exorcising this father obsession and also as a way of moving toward dealing with the mother thing because I am half Swedish. I've been thinking a lot about this and where it's gotten me are my grandmothers. My Swedish grandmother, but especially my English grandmother, well, Irish and Scots from Ontario, actually. She intrigues me. Why did she marry this Chinaman? That's curious to me.

TOSTEVIN: Maybe they were attracted to one another.

WAH: Well, considering the period, that's unusual. I have a feeling it's because my grandfather was a gambler and my grandmother was an ardent Salvation Armyist.

TOSTEVIN: And she was out to save him? [Laughter] While we're on the subject of women, you've said that you were influenced by Quebec women writers. Who and in what way did they influence you?

WAH: The most specific influence was Nicole Brossard. Curiously, the first thing that interested me was her narrative in *A Book*. Not so much a disjunctive narrative but an angular cut, a slicing through the narrative, the fact that she was allowing the short paragraph at the top of the page to constitute the continuity of some kind of narrative. It's really a novel in that it has characters, plot, story, but all of that— the conventional stuff of the novel— is in the background and what's at the forefront is language. I got excited about that because that's what poets do. Well, not all poets, but the ones I'm interested in. Good poetry should bring language to the fore and she was doing it in prose. So I got excited by that and started to read more of her work. It was at a time when Coach House was publishing translations of her work so she was more readily available than other québécois writers. I've looked at others, but not with as much intensity. Talks with Nicole, why she writes the way she writes, have been very generative for me. It confirms the direction I've gone in.

TOSTEVIN: In some interviews, you've mentioned Victor Shklovsky's theory of "making strange" as a technique of art. How does that specifically apply to your writing or to what you were saying about Nicole's influence on your writing?

WAH: What I saw in Nicole, for example, was a way of making strange, and my big take on that has always been out of Keats' "negative capability." How to make use of the negative capability in writing has always been of interest to me. Being able to keep the writing in uncertainty, uncertain of where it's going, its unpredictability. To have that confirmed was a great thing for me.

TOSTEVIN: How does that apply to *Waiting for Saskatchewan*? That book is not only more linear than your other books, it's also very lineal, filial. How do you "make strange" that setting?

WAH: I don't know that it's making that setting strange, or making those people strange. It's using the language... let me contrast it this way. *Grasp the Sparrow's Tail* was published as a small book in Japan and I gave it away to friends, and many of them said, "Gee, this is great, Fred, I really loved it, why don't you write a novel. This would make a great novel," the notion being that this would make a great story. And for about two minutes and thirty-eight seconds, I actually thought of writing a novel.

In other words, what they were getting off on, and people do from that book, is the narrative, the storytelling quality of it.

TOSTEVIN: Do you think that's why *Saskatchewan* won a Governor General's Award, because it is more linear, more storytelling than some of your other writing? [Laughter] Which I think is all pretty terrific, don't get me wrong, but perhaps it would not attract as much attention... [Laughter]

WAH: Yes, George Bowering was on the jury and it was something he could understand... [Laughter] But just a minute. These are heavy questions you're asking. That whole thing of estrangement and making strange...

TOSTEVIN: Well, I don't quite understand... Shklovsky said that the purpose of art is to hold a perception as long as you can. How do you make strange by holding a perception?

WAH: No, you hold the perception by making it strange. He said that the purpose of art was to make the stone stony. We don't pay attention to the fact that the stone is stony. It's a quality that's given, so it doesn't enter our perception. It's not something that we knowingly experience but if I make the stone strange, so that somehow you can experience its stoniness, then there's a perception of something that wasn't there before.

TOSTEVIN: Okay, so I was trying to apply that to *Waiting for Saskatch-ewan*.

WAH: For me it's the poetry, the play, playing around from various angles. Like the *utaniki*— the poetic diary of mixed prose and poetry, and the *Elite* series which explores the division between prose and poetry, and the *haibun*— prose written from a haiku sensibility. Although there's an underlying current of narrative about my father, the prairie, the café, the writing is still intentionally slightly angular because I play at the edges of the poems with language. I have a choice of telling a story about my father and all the restaurants he's been through in his life, in the straightest possible way, or I have the choice of using one long line that goes on and on, as in one of the *Elite* poems, because I want to place that form against the content. I'm interested in play, in invention. To make things strange through negative capability, or whatever means, can be useful to prolong or make something that isn't otherwise available. You twist the forms a bit, like in the prose poems... well that's not really a solid form, but...

TOSTEVIN: Oh I think it's pretty solid...

WAH: Oh, yeah, but formally to describe what a prose poem is, isn't that solid. It's a piece of prose, it's sentences, really.

TOSTEVIN: But it has an energy that traditional poetry, or even poetry using the breath line doesn't always have. The line taken to the edge of the page seems to generate another kind of energy, gives it a certain rhythm that other line breaks don't.

WAH: I discovered that in writing the *utaniki*, the poetic diary. Why should the diary be any less poetic than the poems, and why would the poems be more poetic than the diary? So that in my *utaniki*, *Grasp the Sparrow's Tail*, sometimes the diary entry is made so that it's just as oblique...

TOSTEVIN: So one engenders the other, one is the condition of the other? I like that idea, actually. Speaking of rhythm, you use the word "movement" a lot in your writing and there are many images of movement such as skating, riding, horses, fish in water. I get the feeling when reading you that the environment for such movement— the skating arena, water, etc.— is a mindscape for fluidity in the writing itself. Are you aware of this while writing?

WAH: Yes, although I don't see it as fluidity but as movement. If you want a paradigm for those images that interest me, it's the notion of a plan, a set. The fish, for example. I have a series I'm working on, temporarily called "The Pickerel Series." I'm interested in the spawning fish carrying within itself some map, some imprint it's going to return to all its life. There are three terms that my teacher taught me... but I guess we shouldn't get too theoretical...

TOSTEVIN: Why shouldn't we get theoretical?

WAH: Well, three terms my teacher taught me are *topos*, *tropos* and *typos*. Charles Olson used those terms. *Topos* is place, *tropos*, tropism, is the innate reaction, the movement towards whatever one needs, and *typos* is the typeface, [*slaps thigh*] the imprint on the world that we make or the imprint the world makes on us. So what has always fascinated me, say about hockey, because I played hockey, is the invisibility of the movement. It's moving so fast, and there's that second sense of knowing where to move. Is he going to go there or not, and we're waiting for that moment, that split second to see whether the puck is going to go into the net. It's so nice to have the game fulfil the image.

TOSTEVIN: The way the fish unexpectedly darts around.

WAH: Yes, and the same thing happens when you ride a horse. I've never ridden a horse, except a couple of times, but to ride, you have to have a mind set, a body set, an image of the thing in order to do it. You need to know how to swim before you can swim. I'm interested in the plot, the mass we carry inside ourselves and how this information operates. It's not so much the movement or the fluidity, although that's part of it, but it's the movement and fluidity in fulfilment of some master plan or structure.

TOSTEVIN: So that everything you graph, write, is already in you? There's nothing new?

WAH: Writing for me is simply a way of calling out the information that's already there. Discovering what's there and generating new ways into a world that's already there. You carry with you who you are.

TOSTEVIN: What about the *Pictographs from the Interior of B.C.*? The pictures were already there, they were anterior to your experience. Didn't you come up with something new in the way you read them? Didn't the two together create something new?

WAH: Nothing's new.

TOSTEVIN: There are new ways of tracing, perceiving.

WAH: Okay. They came together and provided a newness for me because it wasn't there before for me, if you see what I'm getting at. I really am more of a Buddhist in all this, I guess... I mean I'm not a practising Buddhist, but there are no beginnings and endings. I love Fenollosa's take on the Chinese written characters for poetry... How false the sentence is as a fabrication, as representation of the world, because nothing in the world ends, nothing ends, so that sentences seem to be such false representations of it. I'm interested in making it new, but it's the same old thing. It's making it new for me, but it's not new, it's already been around. It's the same thing with language. I really love the sense that language carries with it an "emic" structure which is invisible to us but which gets actualized when we use it.

TOSTEVIN: I don't know what you mean by "emic."

WAH: I learned this in linguistics: "eme" as in "phoneme," and "morpheme." We know that there is this invisible "eme" in English that no one can say as a phoneme. I can say the word "ash" in Canada and someone in Buffalo New York will pronounce it "eash" and although they are very close together, they're not the same sounds. I'm not saying that they're speaking a foreign language in Buffalo. When we hear dialects of a language, we know them as dialects, as variations. They are variations of this "eme." Now the only thing that is carrying that "eme" is language. No one person, no one dialect, no one group carries that "eme" for the rest of us. Language carries the "eme." I love the organic nature of language as something that exists outside ourselves and continues to flow through time and space and carries with it all the impedimenta and residue of... of everything. And all languages do that.

TOSTEVIN: So the map, the geography we were talking about at the very beginning, is that a geography of language?

WAH: I don't know what "geography of language" means.

TOSTEVIN: Is the place that you're most comfortable in, language? If your own personal geography is not really Saskatchewan, or any other place you've written about, then does your geography become language?

WAH: Or more accurately, language has become a way of dealing with a geographic "eme" in my cosmology, to use a simile. In other words, you can carry with you who you are, but not be able to tap that or have access to it and language can help you do that. I don't mean only written language, I mean also dance, music, mathematics, painting. These are all languages or ways of showing us what's there.

TOSTEVIN: And you use both paintings and music in your writing.

WAH: I'm not a painter, but I'm a musician. I studied music and played jazz trumpet for many years. A lot of my writing is jazz, just sheer shit jazz. Feels the same way it feels when I play the trumpet.

TOSTEVIN: You've just finished a new series of pieces called *Music at the Heart of Thinking*. How do those pieces relate to music, to jazz?

WAH: They're pushy pieces. They push constantly. Every step of writing in those pieces, every point, is to push it hard so it goes somewhere. Push it fast and force it to move. Don't sit around language, don't sit around word, but at the same time don't fall over, stay on your feet. I love that in music, playing the ad lib in a trumpet solo, or even a group. Trying to keep the piece together and hear the others in the group, how everything is going and push it so hard that it just about falls over the edge and doesn't. Like dissonance, I like the discord because it pushes toward the edge and doesn't fall.

TOSTEVIN: It pushes beyond anecdotes? Beyond story?

WAH: I think so. I have nothing against the anecdote or the story, but I'm pushing beyond so it's not only anecdote or only story. I've done a couple of takes for *Music at the Heart of Thinking* on Frank Davey's last book, *The Abbotsford Guide to India*, which I think is one of his most wonderful books, by the way. It's got story, it's got image, geography, and allows Frank a large spectrum of play. In one of the lines he mentions the random notes on a flute in a hotel lobby. I love the sense of random notes, but you can't have random notes. As soon as you have two notes, they create a structure, a place that is no longer random. What you do when you're a musician or artist is you play the expectation of random-ness against the predictability of form that starts to occur. It's that tension between the two that makes it interesting and it's the estrangement between the two that also makes it interesting. If one goes totally for one over the other, then it gets repetitive and boring. Many artists fall down on that, musically and visually, because they rely purely on formal devices. I fall down on that. Not all of my pieces are successful because they attempt to use form to create form and don't necessarily set up that tension. When a piece works for me, it makes those connections, and takes me to a new place from which language has other possibilities.

TOSTEVIN: I've read *Music at the Heart of Thinking*, and heard you read several pieces from it. They're difficult pieces but they really hook you, and they were very well received at the reading. Why do you think people react so strongly to them? Is there finally a wider acceptance of non-linear, less content-oriented writing in Canada?

WAH: Yeah... Writing is so far behind jazz and painting that way. I was happy that the audience liked them but I was surprised. Again, the technique is to push through the horn so fast and heavy that it goes all over the place but then to have it resolved, have a strong cadence. I think the reason the audience at Harbourfront liked them is that although the poems are oblique, there's something toward the end that brings it together and gives satisfaction to the helter-skelter. They're not that readable off the page, but...

TOSTEVIN: I've read them and I like them a lot. I liked them when you read them as well, because that adds another dimension, the cadence becomes more obvious, but even on the page where meaning totally escapes you at times, they still hook you. I have read some work where meaning escapes you and it gets really boring. I think it was Charles Bernstein who said that much of so-called avant-garde writing done now is just as intrinsically boring as sentimental narrative stories. Both are difficult to do well... This cadence you refer to, is it expressed through the body set you were talking about? Many theorists now emphasize the dual planes at which language operates. Kristeva, for example, sees one of those planes as an instinctual drive such as cadence or rhythm.

WAH: I haven't read much of Kristeva, but it sounds right. I don't know if it's necessarily tied to the body, as much as something that has feeling. It's very musical. Music by and large operates on cadence and I've always been interested in language as a cadential structure, even minutely, in terms of phrases and clauses. How they work cadentially. How a phrase is turned, I'm very curious about that. One of the reasons I've gotten into prose poems in the last few years, particularly in *Music at the Heart of Thinking*, is because I'm more interested in syntax, the syntagm, as a unit of composition, than I am in the line as a unit of composition. Yet both units, the line and the syntagm, require resolution, require movement instead of shape, so I try to break through the syntax, play with it, cut through it, break it up a lot of the time. For about twenty years, I didn't pay much attention to syntax as a poet. I paid more attention to how the line works. My teachers, Creeley and Olson, were line people. Their contribution to changing my perception, at least of how poetry can sound, was through the line, and I was very happy working in the line and still am, but I'm also interested in breaking up other aspects of the poem. Just like the sound poets were interested in breaking up the chronological aspect of writing, playing with that. Nichol's *The Marty-*

rology is a wonderful poem because it does that. If bp feels like breaking up sounds, he breaks up sounds, and if he feels like breaking up sentences he breaks up sentences, and there's this swirl of breaking things up so they can be put back together again, so they can be resolved.

TOSTEVIN: Olson believed that the "I" is always on the move, continually makes itself over again... How do you think that applies to you?

WAH: He did? He said that? I'm not quite sure what that means. What do you think it means?

TOSTEVIN: I'm very much interested in the multiplicity of the selves. I don't believe that there is only one "I" or one subject writing. Kristeva said that whenever you try to define the subject, say a woman, "*ce n'est jamais ça.*" It's never that. It's always on the move toward some other definition. Someone said to me once that it was very important to displace the "I" in writing, and I said, "great, I'll displace it as soon as I find it," because I've never been able to find or define the "I" of my writing as one subject. I see a parallel between Olson's subject continually changing itself and Kristeva's subject-in-process. Are you aware of that process, of that multiplicity, when you're writing?

WAH: I haven't given it much thought. God, Lola, this is a huge question. [Laughter] What is the meaning of Life... [Laughter] Olson said one thing that I've been struggling with all my life. He said that the subjective as objective requires correct processing. Olson's students play around with that all their lives. Sharon Thesen, I think, is a person who really takes that on, the lyric form takes that on. You take that on.

TOSTEVIN: You see me as a lyric poet? Why?

WAH: Because of the "I" in your poems. Lyric poetry is "I"-centred. My point is I haven't concentrated lyrically on the "I." In the *Saskatchewan* book I use the second person as a way of deflecting the I/you.

TOSTEVIN: Yes, but even in using the second person in *Saskatchewan*, there is still a sense of writer being the main subject of that book. Whereas in *Music at the Heart* you don't get that presence.

WAH: I find this very hard to talk about, because I haven't figured it out. It is something that I'm playing with in my poems, the whole notion of the self, of the selves, but I don't know where it's going. It bothers me a little. It seems to have something to do with... Daphne [Marlatt], for example, uses the term "consciousness." I first heard it insisted upon by her. I was really bothered by it. The word "consciousness" doesn't feel like much that's tangible to me, but it's important to her, so I took some trouble to try to experience that word and experience what it meant. She talks about it in reference to proprioception and that makes sense to me. The experience of the "I" as proprioceptive vehicle. Turning ourselves inside out and it's all one skin. The "I" as a kind of surface upon which the rest of the world meets, makes sense to me. The notion of some "I" up here [*points to his head*] has always bothered me, consciousness up here. But Daphne points to herself down here [*points to his stomach*].

TOSTEVIN: Maybe it's a meeting of the two.

WAH: I put consciousness and conscience together and get guilt and thought. Being conscious is being aware...

TOSTEVIN: What does that have to do with guilt? Consciousness and conscience are two separate terms.

WAH: Same root.

TOSTEVIN: I don't believe in the absolute authority of roots or origins. I'm more interested in displacing that authority— I don't know what originary meaning is. Definite definition? Well... let's get back to your work, let's talk about the dream-like quality of some of your images, as when you write that living on the prairies was like living under water. I don't mean dream in the sense of what happens when we're asleep, but in those kinds of images you use to apprehend the world.

WAH: Images are very important to my poetics, images being both pictures and magic. Going back to roots, etymologically, image and magic are connected through that notion of now you see it and now you don't. I'm fascinated by the notion that you can create an image of something in your brain and it becomes true for you. I'm fascinated by the power of the image. I heard wonderful things about cancer therapy that has to do with image-making. I'm frightened to death by the fact that I'm creating cancer for myself, or that I'm creating Alzheimer's for myself. That we do this to ourselves, yet I know we do. How do we control that? I think writers are close to being psychics when they are dealing with images and dreams. I mean, it's not so psychical, or other-worldly. It's not hallucinatory, it's literally part of a world that we can be in. I like to pay attention to that aspect of my writing... the image making. I really hate the term "psychic." What I mean is the literal meaning of the psyche at work.

TOSTEVIN: Are those the images that belong to Lacan's "Imaginary"? Those images that exist before we translate them through the symbolic of language?

WAH: I guess I would agree that we get at them through language constructs.

TOSTEVIN: One depends on the other. Except in our society we have been so preoccupied with the symbolic, language as effective tool, that we have repressed that side of us that makes the images and the rhythms that you were talking about. What I liked about Diana Hartog's book *Candy from Strangers* was how she retains that dream-like quality, the imagery, the Imaginary that is expressed through the Symbolic. They are so well integrated. Perhaps that's why I like *Music at the Heart of Thinking* so much— because it's also well integrated but at another level of play. It's that perfect tension you were talking about. You have the cadence, the rhythm, the feeling and the intellect. I like that.

WAH: Well, I do, too. [Laughter] I think that's me. Music. Heart. Thinking.

TOSTEVIN: It's refreshing to have the thinking part in there as well. Listening to you today, and having read both your poetry and articles, you seem unapologetic about using theory and intellect in your work. I find that in Canada there's a resistance to theory, a reluctance to accept intellectual ideas around writing. Why do you think that is?

WAH: If people bother to read this at all, which they probably won't because it's about Fred Wah by Lola Tostevin, [Laughter] many will cringe at the Olson references. I know that I'm frightened by what I don't know. I've tried to make use of the notion that Olson called "the dance of the intellect"... how does it go... the ear by way of the heart to the line, and the head by way of the syllable... I can't remember the combination... But what it was, was the poetic line as the line to the heart, and the syllable as the threshing floor of the intellect. The two units that one had to pay attention to in poetry: line and syllable. Except, of course, for those writers who continue to think that story is the central feature of our world, exclusively. For me, intellect has always been a dancy thing, something to play with, and that's not usually the way intellect is thought of— as movement, as sparks that fly. The speed of thought. Certainly in *Music at the Heart of Thinking* I'm interested in the relationship between head and hand. A lot of that comes from doing free writing which most people do now. The synapse between thinking something and writing it fascinates me.

TOSTEVIN: Do you do a lot of writing like that? I don't get the impression that *Music at the Heart of Thinking* was written like that. Don't you do a lot of rewrites?

WAH: Every chance I get to change a piece, I'll change it, but I do a lot of writing by hand. I love that sense about the computer, that you can change things so easily. I had problems with a manuscript a few years ago. *Breathin' My Name with a Sigh* was a long poem, so that every time I changed one part of it, it had echo effects and I had to change a number of other pieces in it and it just got too trying to retype it. That's when I got onto the word processor. I've always believed and liked the notion that the author is the authority in the writing, although I don't want to hang that heavily over the writing. Sometimes people have been taken aback that I would change a poem after it's been published and I will. If I have to type something up, send something to somebody, I'll have another go at it.

TOSTEVIN: When you say that the author has the authority over the text, what do you think of reader as the authority over your text?

WAH: Oh, that's getting interesting, too. I'm just starting to think about that. The listener. By and large, I've not thought too much about the reader when I've written. I know the reader is there, that there's a listener at the back of my mind. Who that is has interested me, as a problem in writing. A friend of mine in Calgary, Jackie Fleming, was talking about that, the devaluation of the listener.

TOSTEVIN: Devaluation from whose point of view?

WAH: From everyone's point of view. In the language event, the listener might get it, might not get it, but the speaker/writer is the one who gets it all, so we devalue the role of the listener. She was talking about this as a catholic construct. She's interested in re-evaluating the listener and devaluing the speaker.

TOSTEVIN: Well, there are many theorists who have been interested in making the reader her own writer of the text. Because of the obliqueness and difficulty of a series like *Music*, for example, the reader cannot be passive. Instead of devaluing the reader, it creates another writer. By making her own connections, her own resolutions, the reader becomes the writer of your text.

WAH: Okay. I'm a little curious about the connection, the relationship between the male/female thing. The listener being passive, female, receptacle and the writer being active...

TOSTEVIN: Exactly, but with a series like *Music*, the reader can't be passive, she has to become active, to get anything out of the pieces.

WAH: Oh, absolutely. I want to make the reader pay attention...

TOSTEVIN: It's what Barthes called a writing of seduction versus a writing of conviction. You seduce the reader into taking an active part instead of convincing her to remain passive.

WAH: OOOhhh... I should really read those guys. They confirm everything we do... [Laughter]

TOSTEVIN: You're going to Paris to work on a project. What's the new project you're working on?

WAH: It's a series of poems called "The Gallery Series"— that's the working title, anyway. It has to do with painting, photographs, reading a picture, responding to a picture, translating a picture, dealing with the problems around the artistic and technical problems. I've never had any training in the fine arts, so I don't really know what I'm doing...

TOSTEVIN: That's probably better.

WAH: Yes, it's probably better to know that you don't know what you're doing. [Laughter]

TOSTEVIN: I mean if you're going to come to a painting to transcreate, to read it, as you did with *Pictographs from the Interior of B.C.*, it's best to come to it with no preconceived idea or academic training.

WAH: Yes, I want to use it as a way to learn and train myself about the arts. I'm still very ignorant, especially around painting. I love painting, paintings, but have had problems with technical aspects, such as the frame; the edges are so obvious. I've had problems with the economy of art, it's so expensive. I'm interested in the politics, the Marxist stuff around visual art, and what critics like John Berger have to say. I'm also just plain interested in going to a gallery and giving myself over to a painting that takes me in. There's this big Jackson Pollock painting at the art gallery in Buffalo and when I was a student there I used to go to the Knox pretty often and I always found myself magnetically drawn to this Pollock piece. It was a kind of stock stereotypical Jackson Pollock piece, but it was original and huge and I had expected my reaction to be, oh, well, it's a typical Pollock, it's helter-skelter, then walk away. But I kept going back to that painting until I finally let myself be in it for a while. I love the sense of half-closing the eyes the way you do when you want to see a painting at different angles, give yourself to the sensuousness of the painting. I've never written anything about that and I'm interested in articulating the images that surround that experience. So "The Gallery Series" is allowing me to do a number of things. It's allowing me to play... the form of the pieces is not set. Most of them are line poems so far, not necessarily prose poems. And they are allowing me to find out about the artist. I was thinking how visual art is more distant from its creator than writing because in writing there is usually such a strong identification of authority, but not so much in painting. I've always loved Josef Albers' stuff but I've never let myself write his name. To let yourself write that name in a poem requires a confidence of who that person is in terms of address. Many of the poems address the creator of the art, so that there's a second person in the poems. There's a you who usually made the painting.

TOSTEVIN: It's a different concept from *Pictographs*. You didn't address a "you" in those pieces.

WAH: It's still a transcreational process, however, moving something from one place to another. I'm using the painting as a way of generating the compositional elements that I want in the poem. So that's not so different from *Pictographs*, although there I wasn't concerned about who the author was. There's not that direct an address. But as soon as you ask the question "What does it mean," then you're really asking what the author or artist means. The whole world of meaning has to do with "authority," with author, creator. Compositionally the process isn't that different.

TOSTEVIN: How does that differ from, say, *Waiting for Saskatchewan*? Is that a transcreational process? The images that you were carrying with you.

WAH: Except I wasn't using an object, a representation...

TOSTEVIN: Weren't you using a representation of your father...

WAH: I was using an apparition... I don't mean apparition in any awful or scary sense, I'm always overjoyed when I see him. Wow, there he goes again. But I'm not able to hang on to the apparition long enough to make anything other than the event of "Oh, I keep seeing my father since he's died and what's that all about." So it gets tossed back into a dishing out of memory, of sentimentalism, of nostalgia, working out feelings. It's a much more human or understandable kind of narrative than the playing around that artists do, though I think that playing around gets to be as serious as those stories, as those narratives. *Waiting for Saskatchewan* is biography. My working with painting I don't think is biography. It may become biography, but the working in it isn't.

TOSTEVIN: I find it hard to distinguish between the two. Tracing, graphing, to me can only be biographical. You said yourself before that you write what's already there.

WAH: I don't know... Shirley Neuman is writing a chapter for something on *Waiting for Saskatchewan* as biography. That's why I'm using the term, because it's not a term I usually use, but it made sense what she was saying. *Bio*... I think working with a painting is more *geo*.

TOSTEVIN: We've almost come to the end of the tape and I don't have a final question for you. I'll leave it up to you to say something brilliant.

WAH: Something brilliant... Meaning is everything.

TOSTEVIN: Meaning is everything... What do you mean by that?

WAH: [Laughter] Well, Bowering is always on my ass to make my meaning clear. He's publishing a series called *Errata*, short prose pieces written from the same stance as *Music at the Heart of Thinking*, in a way. But George's at least make sense. [Laughter] I mean you can understand exactly what he's saying and he keeps telling me, "God, Fred, I wish yours made more sense, I wish they were easier to understand," and I keep saying to him, "Well, I agree, George, and I'm going to try harder to make them more understandable to more people."

TOSTEVIN: And are you?

WAH: Oh, I want people to understand, I'm not trying to mystify, subvert meaning...

TOSTEVIN: That's interesting, because you said Nicole influenced you, and she certainly wants to subvert...

WAH: I deny it... I deny it...

TOSTEVIN: You deny it... Well, don't simplify too much...

WAH: God, are you kidding? [Laughter]

Seeking Shape. Seeking Meaning.

Phyllis Webb interviewed by Smaro Kamboureli

Phyllis Webb has had a long career as a poet, but now paints on Salt Spring Island, where she has lived for thirty years. Her most recent books are *Hanging Fire* and *Nothing But Brush Strokes*.

SMARO KAMBOURELI: This is a dialogue about *Hanging Fire*, and I would like to start by asking you about your process of writing the book. You said a number of times that many of the poems in *Hanging Fire*, especially their titles, have to do with words that came to you unbidden. I'd like to hear you talk about where these words come from.

PHYLLIS WEBB: Yes. Well, I'm not really sure where the words come from— that's one of the puzzles, of course, for neurology— I suspect the right brain, although I'm left-handed, so it could be in my case the other way around. They are autonomous words and phrases that simply arrive. I think this is not unusual with writers. They, especially poets, are given rhythmical phrases or curious words to conjure with. And so, while I decided this has always happened to me, I began to be interested in the process. I decided to plot it and watch, and note down, in fact, the words that arrived— if I had a pen and paper handy— and to track this over a period of time to see if there were connections, if there was an underlying preoccupation, perhaps, no matter how disjunctive these arrivals were. It was great fun actually to track these, and often to look up some of them in a dictionary, for instance, and find out that a word would relate back to a previous poem.

KAMBOURELI: A previous poem of yours, you mean.

WEBB: Yes, usually. I'm back at Mount Baker Crescent[1] where this whole thing started and seeing myself sitting there, taking down my words and then playing with them. And this is what I did. I did not want to write, necessarily, rationally on the topic given to me, like, for instance, "Attend," which was a poem that I wrote for Sharon Thesen.

KAMBOURELI: To take this as an example— did you know at the start that "Attend" was going to be a poem responding to Sharon Thesen's work, or to Sharon as the person you are a friend of, or did this correspondence develop later on?

WEBB: I had just read an article by her in which she talked about this process for herself, although she only used the word "attend," as I remember it, that had arrived, and she heard it. So it was a pick-up on that, and that's quite explicable in a very clear connection between reading Sharon's article and then writing the poem for Sharon. But in that poem I explain the process I'm going through and track some words and phrases within it. And they do lead me on, as I say in the poem, they lead me often away, away from what has been given.

KAMBOURELI: In the case of "Attend," you had a specific point of reference to connect the word with. In other cases, though, it's not just a word or an image. It can be an entire sentence or phrase that can be very imagistic or philosophical in its intent. Take, for example, a word like "miasma," or the title of the poem "A Model of the Universe."

WEBB: Or "Anaximander."

KAMBOURELI: Yes, "Anaximander." Or "Eidetic Image" or "Seeking Shape. Seeking Meaning." Do you have a sense of where they come from? I'm not suggesting that there might be a precise source, but I wonder whether these unbidden words are a form of memory that comes to you, a memory residing in the language as it is stored in you.

WEBB: I think that's a good point. They are very often a form of memory or preoccupation. "Seeking Shape. Seeking Meaning," which has a lovely rhythm, really encapsulates a life project.

KAMBOURELI: Could you tell the difference between one of those rhythmical fragments or images that come to you unbidden and other words or thoughts that go through your mind? My reader's instinct tells me that you know the difference, that you know when to respond when that kind of language calls on you.

WEBB: Yes. Well, I noted most of them down, but I didn't work from all of them because some were more suggestive than others and seemed to lead me somewhere. But, also, one of the tests was whether they recurred. "The Salt Tax," for instance, seemed to me totally unpoetic. I just had no entry into the poem that I eventually wrote. But it was so insistent I felt this is a message from the psyche and from my own historical past. So I simply set to work, in that case, and began thinking about Gandhi, and the role he played in my life. Then I read a couple of biographies about him and built up the material. It still seemed really impossible, but by that time I was interested in the subject of Gandhi, and then I heard this music by Philip Glass from *Satyagraha*— that was my lead into it.

KAMBOURELI: Is it this connection with Philip Glass that gave the poem its highly aural/oral qualities, that makes it read almost like a sound poem?

WEBB: Yes, because I was picking up on his repetitiveness, his mono-tonal use of repetitions. They go on in monotones and they are derived from Indian music mainly.

KAMBOURELI: There is an effect of stammering in that poem, too, of delaying the moment of articulation, of hesitancy.

WEBB: Yes.

KAMBOURELI: Repetition as recurrence, but also as struggling, moving through mere sound to syllables and towards meaning— words. Many of the words and phrases in this poem have a certain kind of autonomy in their syllabic-like structure— "this phe-nom—e-non-non..." "a handful of free-ee-dom." This semantic and technical structuring is quite different from your earlier work. You speak of working with dictionary definitions and moving semantically and etymologically from one word to another. But it seems to me that you also locate meaning in pure sound, in the way in which sound engenders meaning or more sounds.

WEBB: I think my quotation from Daphne Marlatt[2] picks up on that idea of sounds attracting meaning. That is why there is a sense of play in a lot of the poems where I'm working from givens. I really did, almost, proceed with exercises, you know, purely associative exercises. Rhyming exercises. As I noted down these things, I would take off on them and do rhymes, and do associations that would lead me on. And so the sounds, for instance— oh, dear— "Cornflowers & Saffron Robes Belittle the Effort." Now this has a wonderful sound to me, and it's rather mysterious in its content. For me it related to Buddhism; it's a very, very tiny poem that's written out of this very long title. I mean long compared to most of the other titles in the book. It's a long sentence to have been given to me. Perhaps, it's untrustworthy in its givenness, but in fact that's what arrived that morning, and so I simply went with sound there. Maybe I should read it. It begins with pure sound:

> Ssh, sigh, silence is coming, the night time blues. Hark.
> Ahem. Sir? I lift my arm, the wind chimes through my
> holy raiment. Mesmeric bells reduce the flies to slum-
> ber. Pajama party. The end of the Raj.

I use some very archaic words in this book, like "alas," "ahoy." They're not totally archaic, but they're not much used— "Hark. Ahem."

KAMBOURELI: Archaic in that they are too poetic, perhaps a bit awkward-sounding to the contemporary reader.

WEBB: Yes. "Ahem" is out of that British tradition of total affectation. And then, "sir," which goes back to the "ssh" sound and "sigh," and "I lift my arm"— and there I'm into an image of wearing something that the wind blows through with holes under the arms (I happen to have a garment like that), and suddenly, you know, there I am with the Buddhist or Hindu. And then the play on "pajama party" and "Raj." So much got caught up in those four lines. It's not a great poem, but it's an interesting compression of thought processes. It's mainly association, this technique I was involved in.

KAMBOURELI: I'd like to go back to a phrase in the passive mode you just used— the insistence on the words having "been given to" you. This implies a passive process for the poet, the poet's ear being a receptacle. It reminds me of the poetics of dictation that Jack Spicer and Robin Blaser talk about. Being dictated, in the verbal sense of the word, as to what to listen to, what to pursue, what to record. I remember George Bowering's opening of *Allophanes* where he begins by reciting a sentence he heard in his mind— in his ear to be exact— in the voice of Spicer— the poet of dictation dictating. What are your thoughts about being initially on the receiver's side, something we might define as passive, before you move into the active mode, the act of construction, of writing?

WEBB: I think that the writer has often felt and feels like a receiver, a receiving station, and so there's nothing extraordinary really about this process, except that I made it conscious and I pursued it and I tried to understand what was going on. I do feel that these givens are totally out of my control, and therefore I am the receptor. But what I do with them is what turns them into the poems. I'm not claiming anything extraordinary about the process.

KAMBOURELI: I was not suggesting that you were. But I do find it extraordinary myself in that through the myriad of words that go through your mind you know which ones to single out and listen to. It was in this context that I found your use of the passive interesting.

WEBB: It's true that I've written about the passivity that I fear about this kind of project. Just waiting around for these things to arrive is passive in itself. But, in a sense, it requires an active attention, and I really concentrated for about two years on paying attention because these things can slip away, and you think, oh, well, or you hardly hear. But I very carefully was attending— that word again— to what was arriving. On some days I would attribute it more to the unconscious than to some muse figure, or something outside myself. I think it's totally within myself and that it is neurologically based. It's combined with memory, I mean it's coming from that data bank, and what the data bank throws up is, goodness knows, controlled by what? I'm sure it has to do with stimuli of the day, of what's on the radio, of what's happening with the weather, of what's happening with my body, and so on.

KAMBOURELI: Would that attentiveness required of you during this process be related to those, almost mythologized, periods of silence you go through in between books? If that's the case, then your reader would have to redefine silence, for it's not a matter of silence but a matter of being actively silent as listener.

WEBB: Yes, and obviously in that fertile silence I am hearing many things and taking in a great deal, so that it doesn't necessarily feel like silence to me. It's just silent from the performance point of view. It requires silence in order to hear, and I suppose that is a very important aspect of the whole process.

KAMBOURELI: "Fertile silence"— it's a wonderful paradox. It reminds me of a point you made in an earlier interview on *Hanging Fire*. You said that you proceed from the irrational in order to create something that makes sense in rational terms. I'm interested in this dialogue between the rational process, if we call it that, by which language manifests itself to you and the very wilful, self-conscious way by which you compose many of these poems. How is this dialogue carried on?

WEBB: I think by putting pen to paper, which is not a very rational process. I mean the rationality is unconscious, if I may put it like that.

Yesterday I put pen to paper, and the phrase yesterday was "speakeasy." It began in a pretty conscious way, and then moved deeper and deeper into connections that I had not expected when I started with the image of the old speakeasy of the 1920s, where one could, I realized finally, speak easy and say what you could not say without the aid of alcohol. It's a wonderful phrase, you know, or word. In fact, I have to be, when I'm writing, in that "speakeasy" frame of mind. It breaks down the inhibitions, and there's always an inner logic to the emotions. I mean there's an emotional logic. And so the scribblings moved from a resentment of inhibition that comes out in this poem in the first four lines or so into the rain forest. Ultimately, it's about the rain forest, but how I got there is not what you'd call a rational process. It's an associative process again that has a rationale because everything connects.

KAMBOURELI: This all echoes, again, your epigraph in *Hanging Fire* from Daphne Marlatt, where she also talks of how words "nudge each other into utterance... a form of thought that is not rational but erotic." Your language has always been very sensuous; it has a sensuality that ranges from the explicit eroticism of such poems as *Naked Poems* to the erotic textures of images and verbal structures that you compose. I find this kind of eroticism to be very strong in many of the poems in *Hanging Fire*, as in "'Krakatoa' and 'Spiritual Storm.'" I'm referring to a certain kind of libidinal energy that has a lot to do, I think, with how you move from the irrational, "given" word to the literal act of writing.

WEBB: One of the things I liked about Daphne's quotation was that she suddenly places the erotic in an almost non-erotic context. It's a "liking," a "drawing," a pulling towards. As if these words liked each other. It's an amusing thought really, that there is this attraction, a magnetic attraction almost, that draws the words and hence the ideas toward each other in this erotic fashion. It seems that this is where my eroticism has gone over these years, into the words, and letting them mate, really, there on the page, and pulling with them oftentimes an erotic context. In "'Krakatoa' and 'Spiritual Storm,'" there is this enormous eruption—

and they always fascinate us; these great volcanic eruptions are terribly exciting. And do you know why? Because emotionally this is a great explosion, an archetype of erotic eruption.

KAMBOURELI: Yes, but I think of eruption in the other sense as well, irruption, Jung's concept of archetypal irruption.

WEBB: I hadn't even thought of that.

KAMBOURELI: The kind of irruption in "'Krakatoa' and 'Spiritual Storm,'" the volcanic eruption, with the lava and the ashes spewing out of the crater, can also be seen as an orgasmic moment, an ejaculation.

WEBB: Oh, yes, I'd forgotten about that one!

KAMBOURELI: This image interests me because you have the earth ejaculating, the female and the male mode coming together, so to speak, another form of liking that resists to an extent some of the gender image assumptions you have in the poem.

WEBB: I have recently been reading a manuscript by Beth Hill about the goddess figure in neolithic times, and there you have the male and the female in one image, the female figure with a penis-like head, a phallic head. She pays a fair amount of attention to this image, which is two in one really.

KAMBOURELI: The phallic mother.

WEBB: The phallic mother, the androgyny. I suppose that volcanic image is kind of bisexual— not bisexual, but androgynous. I was at McMaster University last year where I read this poem to a class. I was asked if I realized how sexual it was, and I said, I thought I *had* realized it because it is extraordinarily sexual for my poetry, which is not that sexual overtly.

KAMBOURELI: It's erotic, too, though. Don't you think that there is a difference between the sexual and the erotic, especially in the way you redefine the erotic in the context of Daphne's quotation? A liking, an attraction, a certain quality of creative energy that makes things happen.

WEBB: It expands the meaning of the erotic, in some ways desexualizes it into this liking, which is a milder form of attraction. It seems a more reasonable thing for words to do.

KAMBOURELI: In a way, then, one might say that this concept of the erotic leads you away from a gender-specific eroticism, and the problems involved in that. But there is, too, an element of violence, a natural kind of cosmic violence that I find also present in other parts of the book, as in "The Way of All Flesh."

WEBB: This violence kept coming up because of what was given. It certainly was part of the revelation. There was revolutionary violence, and anger was one of the undercurrents of the givens that just kept recurring and recurring.

KAMBOURELI: Sometimes you tend to evoke violence in an erotic, often deliberately beautiful or lyrical way— to better alert us to the problems of violence. There is an obvious tension between the lyricism in some of the poems and the violence described in them. I wonder if science is present in these poems because of the scientist's creativity, sometimes a misdirected creativity. It's a kind of creativity that also has female connotations. I remember an article by Evelyn Fox-Keller where she discusses the use of maternal metaphors by nuclear scientists to talk about their post-partum experience after a testing. This appropriation of maternal imagery by the scientific process often results, paradoxically, in—

WEBB: Death.

KAMBOURELI: That's right. What do you think about the creativity of a scientist and that of a poet?

WEBB: I've read enough about the creative process to know that scientists go through a very similar process to artists in making their discoveries. The artist produces a work; they produce a discovery, or theory. I was at the time of writing *Hanging Fire* very interested in physics and was reading all the books that became bestsellers, of course.

KAMBOURELI: Would you like to be more specific?

WEBB: There was *Infinite in All Directions* by Freeman Dyson, and Hawking's *A Brief History of Time*. I'd done some reading about string theory (which gets into "A Model of the Universe"). I remember typing out a long passage on that from *The Second Creation: Makers of the Revolution in 20th Century Physics*. Another was called simply *Entropy*. Sometimes I just dipped into them for plunder–metaphor hunting. In "Long Suffering" I refer to those "butterflies whose effects are infinite"— straight out of James Gleick's *Chaos*, for which I'm eternally grateful. Recently I've been compulsively watching *Star Trek: The Next Generation*! And playing against this cosmological vastness is the activity of experimental scientists in their labs. Those two worlds collide where the use of animals in experimentation is horrendous. This is one of the themes in the book. I'm very concerned with animal rights. I have a great respect for the animal kingdom. That's where the moral problems are posited, right there in the lab, with the animals being hurt for our benefit. This comes up in my poem "Anaximander" where I saw Anaximander as one of the first scientists in that tradition of analysis, of breaking down, of intruding in, of intervening in the processes of life. That accounts for the little paragraph about Doctor Melzack whom I knew and in whose department I worked as secretary many long years ago. That's where I saw the cat with the electrodes on its head. I was talking to a friend of mine the other day, who has AIDS, and he always says how grateful he is for the medicine, and every time he says that I see the animals. And I am grateful he has the medications, but the big, ethical question is who has the right to life. Just because we're bigger and stronger and have the tools and so on, we seem to think we have. It's immoral; it's a continuing problem.

KAMBOURELI: Is this part of the dilemma in the "Yes. No" in "Anaximander" and in the paradigm shift you're talking about?

WEBB: I think the big paradigm shift in our culture right now is the feminist shift, the shift into the realization of the feminine point of view, experience, and theory. That is only one. There are so many paradigm shifts going on that we are in a great whirl. I mean W-H-I-R-L. Feminism is a profound paradigm shift. I don't know if it's even been ever mentioned as one, but we are in the throes of it. The other, of course, is the environmental shift, where we, in order to survive, must change our vision from centering on the human-centered to the animal- and environment-centered view of the world. That is what Olson in fact posited in "Projective Verse," that our egos must shrink.

KAMBOURELI: One of the things I find fascinating about you is that I know you to be a very self-conscious feminist in your everyday life, but when it comes down to print you tend to skirt the issue. I have in mind your wonderful essay "Message Machine," in *Language in Her Eye*. Feminism and gender issues are present in it, as they are in your poetry too, but in an oblique, almost subliminal way. You don't always thematize these issues in a direct fashion. Is there a specific reason for this?

WEBB: Well, I'm uncomfortable with dogma. I was recently accosted in Essen, Germany, by a young man who rather accusingly said, you didn't mention anything about feminism. I felt that the poems could speak for themselves. But I think I thematize it in my poem in *Hanging Fire*, called "The Making of a Japanese Print." It just creeps up and develops in the poem, and is stated at the end. That is, I think, my most overt statement. But I just don't want, in fact I'm bored with, a programmatic approach to anything. I mean there's not a very thematic approach to anything in my work. I like it to sneak in with its emotive power, rather than to be laid on. When I wrote "Message Machine," I was really dealing with something in myself, which is contra-active, and passive— this process of listening and not taking, in a sense, responsibility for what's happening in my head. I felt I was dealing in a slightly amusing way with the whole problem of passivity in women. Actually, more in myself than in "women," in my writing process, because I think in order to write you have to lie back, you have to rest, and often lying down is for me literally lying down.

KAMBOURELI: The horizontal position.

WEBB: The horizontal position— laid back, right?— allows the entry of words.

KAMBOURELI: *There* is a sexual metaphor again.

WEBB: It embarrasses me that I have to admit to this supine position. So I was dealing with embarrassment in view of the theoretical feminist stance of the book. I guess I'm trying to deal with my resistance to theory, my resistance to programs, my resistance to dogma and correct thinking. And so I do it via the means of humour, mainly, and lightheartedness. As I've become older, I have become less patient with rhetoric. When I became a consciously politicized person, when I was seventeen or so, rhetoric was fine with me. It was very useful in political work. But I don't want to be conned, I don't want to be seduced by programmatic orders. It is a very personal resistance to being one of the group.

KAMBOURELI: What would the group be in this case?

WEBB: I guess it would be the feminist group. It would be the cause—

KAMBOURELI: But it's so diverse, though. Can we really talk about *the* group?

WEBB: Yes, of course, it is diverse. I mean I am a feminist, I am part of the group, but I still have a lot of resistance.

KAMBOURELI: You don't want to be framed or labelled.

WEBB: No, I've never wanted to be framed or labelled. That's part of my mysterious moving.

KAMBOURELI: I'm glad you've used this word mysterious because it fits my sense of you, the way you move around, your process of writing. but at the same time that you're engaged in this mysterious, if you want, psychic process— the way your images and poems are engendered— there is also a very strong tendency in your work, especially in this recent book, to move towards the referential world where all kinds of struggles occur. I'm thinking of "The Salt Tax" and of more intimate poems like those you wrote about the deaths of Gwendolyn MacEwen and Bronwen Wallace, and of other poems dealing with large political issues.

WEBB: "You Have My Approval," which is about terrorist directives.

KAMBOURELI: Exactly. I see a very interesting, not necessarily paradoxical, dialogue between the psychic and the tangible worlds.

WEBB: And political world.

KAMBOURELI: Yes. Your engagement with power structures, your concern both with negative forms of power and power in the sense of being empowered to act in a performative way, making something happen— this has always been present in your work.

WEBB: Actually, I act less and less in a performative way—

KAMBOURELI: But the writing—

WEBB: The writing is doing it more. I would like to make a comment here about that and the process, this passive process of awaiting the words, listening for the words, and then writing from them, responding to them, that it led me so much outward. This very inward, private process, led me more and more outside. It connected me, it associated me with the outside world.

KAMBOURELI: I see this in the way you transform all those things that are part of the malaise of our culture— TV, various aspects of consumerism or of totalitarian systems, what you call the sleazy world, the Pharmasave— into something else. You don't necessarily find a saving grace in them, but you employ them creatively. I'm thinking, for instance, of "Paradise Island."

WEBB: I think that many other poets do this all the time, working with the realist tradition. I'm thinking at the moment particularly of Patrick Lane and Lorna Crozier, Leona Gom, and Bronwen Wallace, who are or were working very much out of a realist and narrative tradition. This is not my mode, normally. In the case of "Paradise Island"— this episode which happened and the despair of this woman so upset me that it threw me into that nexus of goods. I felt really compelled to say something about it because the talk around was that it was a great joke, that, aha! you know, the Pharmasave was held up! She didn't even have a gun; she got what she wanted until the RCMP arrived. It was, I suppose, something about my own suicidal past and even present that was touched by this story. Also, the despair of poverty. It encapsulated so much about women's condition in our society if they have no power, if they are poor, if they are emotionally desperate. That awful Pharmasave was the stage for this drama, which was perceived as a comedy, and which I saw as a tragedy. I was just moved into that, that world of everyday reality.

KAMBOURELI: So there is, to some extent, a redemptive potential in this story because you create an affirmative poem out of this incident. Not to mention the name of the place itself— pharma (poison, cure) and save. You've written before about similar kinds of despair and about death, but I think that in this book you treat negativism in a different way. I'm thinking of the Japanese print poem where the woman in the print is almost frozen, a silent figure. In someone else's creation, but in your poem, which is, fittingly, I think, the last poem in the book, she comes alive, madly alive, because you give her a voice by giving her a poem.

WEBB: She's swearing. I mean I'm swearing. I realize that I am that woman. The cool, factitious, apparently pleasing woman, with the fan in my hand.

KAMBOURELI: The damned fan.

WEBB: The damned fan. She took a long time to emerge, that woman, cursing, because I have only recently learned how to do that in my work. I've done it in my life, but I have not been able to get it into the work until recently. I think that's a big advance in *Hanging Fire*, that my anger really comes through, and I'm able to curse.

KAMBOURELI: What has made it possible for you to let this anger surface in this book?

WEBB: I attribute it to the many feminist angry young women poets whom I've mentioned before. They gave me the sign, the sign that my time had come to be freer. I think that's certainly one of the major influences. And it's interesting that, as I get older, my influences get younger. As I always say, younger and wiser.

KAMBOURELI: Would you like to mention some of these younger women writers.

WEBB: Well, Bronwen Wallace, Di Brandt, Mary Melfi who inspired one of my poems in *Water and Light*, and a lot of the prose writers, too. Sharon Thesen, too, who has a wonderful way of handling anger in her poems but still maintains a lyric quality. I'm not particularly interested in maintaining the lyric any more, and I felt in this book that I did not. And it's not just the anger. It's a widening of the subject matter, an opening up of the domestic material, in part, where of course a lot of the violence occurs. In my life, the domestic violence has not been in my adult life so much as in my childhood life. Violence was certainly there. I suppose I don't have that much to lose any more. There is a general accessibility now to the unspoken. For most of my life, many things were not spoken about but are now so freely that my writing, I imagine, seems pretty mild to the young writers or readers. I don't know.

KAMBOURELI: These writers that you call young writers, though, tend to be more realistic in their writing than you are.

WEBB: Yes, they do, except for Sharon.

KAMBOURELI: Also, your work doesn't have the kind of domesticity we find in Bronwen's or Leona's work, for example. I can only remember your kitchen poem from *Water and Light* as one poem that might be defined as domestic.

WEBB: That's one poem which is constantly quoted as my feminist statement, and I'm glad I made it. My life is not traditionally domestic in the sense that there is a family; there is no family; there is no husband. I don't have that many referents, and it has been deliberately designed in that way. But because that whole area has been opened up as a subject for poetry, I suppose it's just giving me more access to the revelations that came with opening up, a freedom of expression that I didn't feel before was available.

KAMBOURELI: I'd like to talk a little bit about the design of the book. Although many of the poems came on their own, and you composed them independently of each other, they hang together. There is a strong element of linkage in the book, the book as a gathering.

WEBB: I thought of it as a book. In fact, I thought it would all be poems out of this process that we talked about, but I decided to include some poems from the past that I hadn't gathered together in a book. These appear in the last section, "Scattered Effects." Originally, I conceived the book as five-partite, but then realized that was unnecessary and that it really fell into three parts. Some poems got taken out of the first part, "Tour de Force," and placed elsewhere once I established a three-part structure. "Scattered Effects" is really scattered, and yet it works quite well as a separate section. "Hanging Fire," the middle section, is the one that gathers the political material together. Once I got into the Lenin poems, the others seemed to drape themselves around the concrete poems. The journal piece, "To the Finland Station," supports the thematic material about fire and revolution; and then, the Salman Rushdie poem, too, seemed to exemplify the whole idea of hanging fire and holding back the fire in a sort of terrifying way. I think that the first part was showing off the variety of forms I was using. I was playing with the idea of force, of course.

KAMBOURELI: You mentioned the variety of forms in the book. One of them is that of the prose poem. I wonder whether you're turning to prose in this book because prose might be a more appropriate form of discourse for our time, or you just wanted to explore the prose poem form.

WEBB: I started writing prose poems because the subject matter required it. I was also enjoying very much just using sentences. I think in the prose poem you're so much more aware of manipulating the sentence and its varieties.

KAMBOURELI: Yes, but even in some of the non-prose poems, the sentence as a unit seems to play an important role. I'm thinking, for example, of "You Have My Approval": "Turn the turtle over. Test its white stomach./Find your island. Find the treasure."

WEBB: Perhaps I finally expanded my line as I had wanted to do many years ago. I was simply, I think, moving freely between prose and poetry. And then I began trying to understand why there are so many prose poems being written right now, and then I got into my paradigm shift idea. I felt I trusted my writing, doing prose, I mean, because I don't usually trust prose that much for myself. I found I really enjoyed writing these little pieces.

KAMBOURELI: Do you see a difference between the prose poem and the poet's prose?

WEBB: Yes, yes. You're not trying to do the same thing. When I write prose, I usually try to write logically and proceed in an understandable fashion; whereas in the prose poem I'm deliberately upsetting logical expectations.

KAMBOURELI: I was thinking of your "Message Machine," an essay that is very poetically constructed, where you actually record your process of writing it as you write about something else. This self-reflexive process appears as a frequent motif in *Hanging Fire*. There are many points in this book where you thematize the writing act as it occurs. Do you associate this kind of self-reflexivity with the resistance to the lyric form that is so noticeable in this book?

WEBB: The middle section, "Hanging Fire," is, among other things, about the death of the lyric poem and my sense that that comes out of the kind of world we live in. That we are not in a Wordsworth land any more, and that even those who write what are called lyric poems are treating their subject matter very differently from the old lyric. In a sense, there are very few true lyrics being written any more. I'm not just talking about my own work here where I'm deliberately letting the lyric go (and this also accounts for the prose poems) but feeling in the face of our social conditions that the lyric response is almost impossible. I mean people still fall in love, but the kind of stuff they write about isn't very often lyrical. I guess love was one of the main themes of lyric poetry— and nature, and we can't be that lyrical about nature, either. I love to hear a lyric voice, and I suppose it's still there in some of my work. But I was not setting out to write a musical book. I call these poems my uglies.

KAMBOURELI: Your uglies! I remember you saying that you left behind the pure poetic voice and are moving now into "ugly poetry." Don't you think, though, you'd have to redefine what ugly is? Is this another paradigm shift from the aesthetic to the anti-aesthetic, a distrust of purity or of the subjective condition of beauty?

WEBB: I think it is. It's also part of wanting to be slightly offensive. And

I have never, I think, challenged in an experimental way, very profoundly, in a way that might upset and disconcert. I've always worked within certain parameters that are more or less acceptable, although I've done, you know, my own experiments, but nothing really very wild or new or original. That might be an aspect of the whole idea of pleasing, which I found was one of those ideas that kept coming up again and again. I wrote this book realizing just how much women are trained to please and how much I've been trained to please and how this modifies my behaviour, my poetic behaviour. So I'm well-behaved. Always the good daughter. Yes, I think I'm a fairly well-behaved poet.

KAMBOURELI: Would this relate to your sense of readership, of audience? Do you have a specific kind of reader in mind for this book, a reader you'd like to upset, disturb, a little?

WEBB: I may be, in some sense, courting a younger audience by doing this, although I don't know if they're interested. But then I realize that they don't know about Lenin's speech of 1917 at the Finland Station; that would appeal to old revolutionaries or, you know, revisionists, those who know history. Since there isn't much of an audience for poetry, I suppose one is a bit irresponsible in imagining an audience. I just felt that this was a transition book. For one thing, all my books are transitional, but this one in particular. I felt that I was in between. I was doing the prose but wasn't sure about it— am I going into prose or is this just the mood of the times?

KAMBOURELI: This kind of question is raised formally by many of the poems in the book. The voice in some of the prose poems is not exactly that of speech or conversation. There is a strong sense of poeticality about it that, perhaps, has to do with the primacy of the sound effects in these poems. So you're not moving into prose as prose; it's not such a radical departure from the lyric voice in terms of the melodious qualities we associate with the lyric. Your undoing of the lyric is done ever so subtly.

WEBB: I pay a great deal of attention to sound. I think that, although "The Making of a Japanese Print" is a transitional poem, I achieve there some sonic effects that are quite beautiful, like, "Then washy blue three-quarters up." I love that. Yes, perhaps there is more attention to sound than sense, particularly in the first section.

KAMBOURELI: I think that by resisting the lyric you also resist a certain kind of closure, the lyrical ending that is part of the whole lyric tradition, romantic or not. Think, for instance, of "A Model of the Universe," where you begin the last stanza in the conditional mode, but that conditional structure is not completed, just hangs there, the gap at the end being emphasized by the ellipses.

WEBB: I cannot bear to finish that thought. Yes, and it also happens in the Hopkins poem where it's definitely anti-climactic, although it is a very joyful poem.

KAMBOURELI: What does this resistance to closure suggest?

WEBB: It partly comes out of my adherence to the modernist approach as developed by the old boys— leaving the poem open for the reader to participate in and all those clichés (they are clichés now, I guess), not wanting the neat or the dramatic or the high-sounding ending. Occasionally, I give in to that. Sometimes I think it's required to snap the poems shut. It occurs in the slightly witty poem, "Cat and Mouse Game," that ends with a rather snappy line. But another poem, "As Rare as Hen's Teeth," declines, and yet it declines into an open-ending that also has a closure. It's truly open-ended, but emotionally closed. It's not much of an ending, not an ending with a bang. It's a really whimpering ending. Emotionally, though, it's final.

KAMBOURELI: The other thing that stands out in these poems is how, where, the "I" is situated. I noticed that quite often the "I" appears late in a poem, and that it's not necessarily identical to the lyric ego, that there is a difference between the speaking voice and the voice of Phyllis

Webb. Is this related to the anti-lyric elements in this work, to a resistance to the internalized subjectivity of the lyric?

WEBB: "Ambrosia" has a disruptive "I," really, the "I" of the unbeliever who is actually caught up in this ambrosial moment of writing the poem about Hopkins. It's echoing, of course, "I am so happy, so happy," which were Hopkins' last words. These words become mine. And yet I'm still very separate from him. So I don't know if that's part of the anti-lyric, although I think it might be in this poem.

KAMBOURELI: The "I" also appears to be in some poems in a passive, or rather suspended position— "I sit on a rock."

WEBB: Oh, yes, I sit, right.

KAMBOURELI: Yet on other occasions the "I" is a moving "I" because the poet figures there as a tourist, as in the journal poem and in the Krakatoa poem. I like this tension between stasis and motion, and also the ecstatic moments that appear elsewhere in the book where the "I" is decentred in the sense that an image or word sends you to a different site of truth from the one you're at. So there are many "I"s.

WEBB: "Performance" has another one of those "I"s. The I-narrator can be distant from the event. I mean in "Krakatoa" that is so. I am the "I" explicitly there. And the "I" in "Anaximander." I'm having a smile here because I have the male philosophical tradition with its grand theories and its cosmological adventures, and then I deliberately cramp it down into this little thing, sitting on the rock in the wood, studying the moss. This poem has a kind of dialectical movement. For me it's slightly humorous. I'm minimizing myself in this poem into this little hummingbird. That's what the "I" is doing there. It plays against the lot— the geographer, the cosmologist, the inventor, the philosopher. In a sense, it's a feminist revolt against the male intellect.

KAMBOURELI: It's a feminist subversive gesture, studying moss, that— do I dare use this word— deconstructs—

WEBB: Yes, yes!

KAMBOURELI: — the grand design of established cosmologies. What you do is look around at the immediate world and discover a microcosm that might be as grand as the grandest systems of philosophy ever invented. It's a matter of questioning those principles by which we privilege a condition always at the expense of another.

WEBB: Gerry Gilbert has a little prayer-like line that goes "make me see closer and smaller." I love that line because I take it as an instruction for good writing. What I've noticed about the tired mind is that it ceases to see close up. In a way, that is what "As Rare as Hen's Teeth" is about— those clichés that come when the mind is tired and not seeing accurately any more.

KAMBOURELI: "Performance," with its "I infesting my poems," is intriguing because it both opens with the "I" and it questions the "I's" performance. There is some kind of a festering wound in this poem that has to do, I think, with the condition of the "I."

WEBB: That's neurosis. You may have noticed that neurotic people are often absorbed in themselves. It's like a sickness. I think that's part of the reference in the poem. There is a neurotic self-absorption which is part of the sickness, a symptom of sickness. I suppose my early work might be construed this way. And was. But, try as one might, one cannot get rid of the "I." At least, I can't. I think that's why I do so much dancing around with the "I," and was concerned with the lyric and the function of the first-person singular. In a sense, this ties up with the other questions about the death of the lyric poem. This poem is so loaded with "I"s, but it is certainly tangling with all the possible functions of the first person.

KAMBOURELI: The "I" here becomes pluralized.

WEBB: I, we. I is. It becomes more noun-like, much more object-like, or other.

KAMBOURELI: The other thing that's interesting in this poem is the notion of performance itself, the self performing or the poet performing in terms of the writing act, but also performance in the sense of the poet actually performing in front of an audience.

WEBB: I had to read at an Amnesty reading in Victoria. I wrote this poem to have something new to read. So "the performing whales" also get into it, and Amnesty being concerned with prisoners, I was concerned with whales as well. Actually, it's almost a conceit. I was writing a poem about performing the poem I was writing. The whole connection with the audience was definitely the main concern— apart from working out the role of the first-person singular. But the performance was not so much about the writing performance, though that's in there, as the performance performance. I just couldn't resist playing with the idea of the audience. I must say the first reading went very well. It's much better read than read in a book.

KAMBOURELI: One of its last lines, "I am only a partial fiction," is very intriguing. It brings up questions about the autobiographical self and reminds me of Rimbaud's "je est un atre" ("I is an other"). I wonder what you have in mind here with respect to the "I" speaking and the act of constructing a fiction.

WEBB: I don't know that it's possible to be anything but at least partly fictional when you're writing. It is not life, it is writing. So there is no way this "I" can be totally me. It's an artifact, a fiction, but there is enough truth, at least in "Performance": there I am, standing up, reading the poem to the audience, and that's me.

KAMBOURELI: To some extent, then, you're almost addressing the fundamental mystery of otherness, if I can call it that for a minute, but you also demystify this otherness by presenting a much more direct, more easily accessible or recognizable self.

WEBB: It sounds lovely.

KAMBOURELI: In "Performance," you meditate on the many guises of the self in a reflexive and whimsical way— the self as an interior construct, as voice, as body. Ironically, though, the journal poem, which is written in a more directly autobiographical style, was written, as I understand, much later than the time at which the events described in it occurred. It is a fictionalized autobiographical moment, a reconstruction.

WEBB: The incidents are true but it was a wonderful exercise in concentration, in reliving those few days. To reconstruct it in language that would sound like the real thing. I felt almost like a novelist for a few days.

KAMBOURELI: In the second section of the book, besides the noticeable, and often visible, changes in style and form, there is too your long-standing fascination with things Soviet, the revolution specifically. I wonder what the impact of the recent changes in the Soviet Union would be on your writing, for that material seems, at least to me, to go beyond history for you; it has become part of your imaginative centre.

WEBB: Although my political temptation to become a communist goes way back to when I was an undergraduate, I don't think I was particularly fascinated by Lenin as a figure then. My attraction was much more theoretical. This concern with Lenin is much more recent, and I don't know how to account for it. As I say in "To the Finland Station," "why this obsession with Lenin?" In a way, I answered these questions in the poem.

KAMBOURELI: The Lenin seen in the poem is a kind of domesticated figure. The great political man is certainly there, but in the background. In the foreground, there is Lenin the artist figure, especially as he comes across in the concrete poem, "Lenin Skating."

WEBB: I was charmed when I first discovered that he was a figure skater, Lenin as young artist and creator of the future. That in part is my fascination with Lenin. In a way it deflated the exaggerated statuesque person, and demoted him somewhat to know that he had this freedom of movement at one time, then moved into this totally statuesque figure in our history. I mean he has been immobilized by history and by the future. He became concretized after he died.

KAMBOURELI: Yes, and literally, too. It's been interesting watching on television all those statues of Lenin falling down to pieces— like the Berlin wall.

WEBB: That's right. Why not, then, a concrete poem for a concrete figure? But I'm not sure where my sort of mystical sense of belonging to Russia comes from. Perhaps I'll never know that. It is simply a very deep emotional feeling that I have, that has grown over the years. I've only been there twice. If it has to go with past lives, if I believed in that or not, it could do. It also has a great deal to do with my utopian visions when I was younger. It was a struggle to enter and then have to reject that dream of a just society. It's also part of the whole disconnecting from the patriarchal tradition. In a sense, I'm deconstructing Lenin in the concrete poem, "Mother Russia."

KAMBOURELI: Lenin, and also the master narrative he has come to represent. You tend to do that a lot— work within a certain master narrative but at the same time doing so by undermining it. I'd like us to talk about another poem, too, one of my favourite poems in the book, "Self City."

WEBB: It's one of mine, too. Do you know it came out of you showing me that postcard of Prague?

KAMBOURELI: Yes. I went to Prague looking for Kafka, and I found him completely by accident. That was before the "velvet" revolution. But one of the things that intrigues me about this poem is its title. It suggests a gathering of disparate elements that come together in various configurations. There is a sense of plenitude in the book— all the directions you move in— but at the same time this plenitude is not necessarily of a paradisal kind. You seem to alert us to the dangers involved in having plenitude— "the egoless Transcendent/poised on the parapet,/armed & dangerous"— and you shift from your high-priest-ess mood or voice that appears in your earlier work to a voice that gives in to an apocalyptic vision that is also distrusted.

WEBB: I was thinking of the great intellectual constructs that appear to be egoless, including the communist doctrine, the objective scientist outside of the experiment, although we know now that the observer is always part of the experiment. I wrote this poem before I wrote my journal entry in "To the Finland Station," where I talk about the armed guards of the parapet, which links very nicely with "Self City." That was quite a powerful image for me as we sat at the station at the border. It was quite a fearful moment just because there is so much associated with that situation. I believe one has to honour the ego and admit that it is part of everything we do, and not pretend that we are egoless beings unless we are Buddhists of the highest order.

KAMBOURELI: What kind of connection do you see between the "I" that we talked of earlier and the ego?

WEBB: It all depends. I think the "I" has to come out of the ego.

KAMBOURELI: It is, then, a specific articulation of the ego.

WEBB: Yes, but depending on whether it is more or less a persona, whether it's your own ego or not, or an "I" appropriate for the situation.

KAMBOURELI: You have a line in the book about "the mind of the poet." Where is the mind situated in relation to the ego?

WEBB: The mind does not have a lot to do with the ego in the way I was writing these poems.

KAMBOURELI: So the dictionary of that kind of mind would not necessarily be a verbal kind of dictionary, but a dictionary of psychic, pre-verbal language. Is this then, related to other poems, like "Seeking

Shape. Seeking Meaning," where you talk about the syntax of deep structure?

WEBB: Yes, because deep structure is again a kind of archetypal mode, but almost implanted like an instinct in birds. The mind understands deep structure and creates language with that knowledge.

KAMBOURELI: So surface structure would suggest a more pheno-menological approach to language.

WEBB: I think so.

KAMBOURELI: It's interesting that you use language as metaphor to talk about deep structure as the site of the unconscious, as that psychic centre of energy that is total anguish.

WEBB: What else do we have? And the stringing along means not paying too much attention to rational meanings.

KAMBOURELI: "Hanging Fire"— as the title of the entire book and of its middle section and of a poem in that section— reinforces the fire imagery in the book.

WEBB: It's a multi-layered image. Many of the fire images are quite negative. I had the initial theme of hanging fire and then this sort of vision of a curtain of fire— mainly, I guess, associated with the bombing of Dresden.

KAMBOURELI: Your fire imagery made me think of Canetti's *Auto da Fe*, and that erudite professor who burns his incredible collection of books, thus extinguishing, in a way, who he is.

WEBB: I actually did write a poem about the Nazi book burnings, and I thought about including it. I wrote it a long time ago but I decided not to include it. It's interesting that your mind goes to that idea. But it wasn't a good poem, so I didn't include it. Book burning, though, was part of the imagery for myself. And then, of course, it connects to the poem dedicated to Salman Rushdie, "You Are Nowhere." "Mind is shapely. Art is shapely"— as Ginsberg says and as I quote him in "Seeking Shape. Seeking Meaning." I think we must trust that primal creativity, trust its slow-motion urge toward order and enlightenment.

NOTES

My thanks to Kristin McPeek and Craig Burnett for the transcription, and to Evelyn Cobley for her photographs.

1. Her house on Salt Spring Island between 1987 and 1989.
2. This quotation, an excerpt from "musing with mothertongue," is the epigraph to *Hanging Fire*: "in poetry... sound will initiate thought by a process of association; words call each other up, evoke each other, provoke each other, nudge each other into utterance... a form of thought that is not rational but erotic because it works by attraction... a drawing, a pulling toward, a 'liking.'"

Notes on the Contributors

MARK ABLEY was born in England and raised in Alberta and Saskatchewan. He has published his poetry widely, and is the author of several books, including *Glasburyon*, and *The Ice Storm*. He lives in Montreal.

LUCY BASHFORD lives in Victoria, B.C. where she is Assistant Editor at *The Malahat Review*.

BRENDA CARR lives and teaches in London, Ontario.

JOHN LIVINGSTONE CLARK was born on Salt Spring Island, British Columbia, and has lived in Saskatoon since 1984. His books of poetry include *Passage into Indigo, Breakfast of the Magi*, and *Prayers and Other Unfinished Letters*. He has published prose in various journals, including *Canadian Fiction Magazine*.

BEVERLEY DAURIO is the author of three books, including *Hell & Other Novels*, and has edited more than 100 titles, including *Dream Elevators*.

SMARO KAMBOURELI's most recent book is *Scandalous Bodies: Diasporic Literature* in English Canada. She is a Professor of Canadian literature in the English Department, University of Victoria.

BRUCE MEYER is Director of the Writing and Literature Program at the University of Toronto School of Continuing Studies. He has published sixteen books, including four collections of poetry: *The Open Room, Radio Silence, The Presence* and *Anywhere*; the short fiction collection *Goodbye Mr. Spalding*; two volumes of interviews, *In Their Words* and *Lives and Works*; and two textbooks, *The Stories* and *The Reader*. A frequent broadcaster on CBC's *This Morning*, he is also author of *The Golden Thread: A Reader's Journey through the Great Books*.

ROY MIKI is the author of *The Prepoetics of Williams Carlos Williams: Kora in Hell* (UMI Research Press), *A Record of Writing: An Annotated and Illustrated Bibliography of George Bowering* (Talonbooks), *Saving Face: Selected Poems 1976-1988* (Turnstone), With Cassandra Kobayashi, *Justice in Our Time: The Japanese Canadian Redress Settlement* (Talonbooks/National Association of Japanese Canadians), *Market Rinse* (DisOrientation Chapbooks), *Random Access File* (Red Deer College Press), *Broken Entries: Race. Subjectivity. Writing.* (Mercury), and the forthcoming collection of poems, *Surrender* (Mercury). He is also an editor, scholar, and activist, and lives in Vancouver, B.C.

BRIAN O'RIORDAN is currently Vice-President of G.P. Murray Research Ltd. of Toronto. He has co-authored with Bruce Meyer two books of interviews with Canadian writers, *In Their Words* (1985) and *Lives and Works* (1991), and has contributed poetry, reviews and articles to many literary journals in Canada.

MONTY REID lives and works in Ottawa.

JAY RUZESKY's books include *Writing on the Wall* and *Painting the Yellow House Blue*. He edited a special issue of *The Malahat Review* on P.K. Page (#117) to celebrate her 80th birthday.

Montreal poet, painter and publisher SONJA A. SKARSTEDT's third poetry collection, *Beautiful Chaos* (Empyreal) was just released. Also due in 2000: her first play, *Saint Francis of Esplanade*, and a novel for young readers.

ROBERT SWARD is winner of a Guggenheim Fellowship, the author of twelve books, including *A Much-Married Man*, a novel, and *Four Incarnations: New & Selected Poems*, published by Coffee House Press. Lucille Clifton selected Sward for a Villa Montalvo Literary Arts Award, and his fiction has been heard on National Public Radio's "The Sound of Writing." Sward currently teaches for Cabrillo College and the University of California Extension in Santa Cruz.

LOLA LEMIRE TOSTEVIN is the author of five books of poetry, *Color of Her Speech, Gyno-Text, Double Standards, 'sophie,* and *Cartouches*, a novel, *Frog Moon*, a collection of essays, *Subject to Criticism*, and of a new novel to be released in 2000. She lives and works in Toronto.

Notes on the Interviews

Margaret Atwood interviewed by Mark Abley: the interview originally appeared in *Poetry Canada Review*, 15:2, 1995.

Leonard Cohen interviewed by Robert Sward: the interview took place in Montreal, Quebec, in 1984. Copyright 1984, 1998, by Robert Sward. Used by permission.

Lorna Crozier interviewed by Bruce Meyer and Brian O'Riordan: this interview was conducted while Lorna Crozier was visiting Toronto in March 1988 and additional information was gained during our visit to Saskatchewan in December, 1988, and originally appeared in *Poetry Canada Review*, 10:1.

Claire Harris interviewed by Monty Reid. Reprinted with permission. Originally published in *Waves: Fine Canadian Writing*, 13: 1, 1984.

Michael Harris interviewed by Sonja A. Skarstedt: the interview originally appeared in *Poetry Canada Review*, 11:2.

Roy Kiyooka interviewed by Roy Miki: the interview took place at Roy Kiyooka's Powell Street studio in the early afternoon of July 4th, 1978, amid the steady hum of city traffic.

Daphne Marlatt interviewed by Brenda Carr: the interview was originally published in *West Coast Line*, 25:1, 1991.

Gwendolyn MacEwen interviewed by Robert Sward: the interview was done in Toronto in 1986.

Erin Mouré interviewed by Beverley Daurio: the interview took place by mail and was originally published in *Books in Canada*.

P.K. Page interviewed by Lucy Bashford and Jay Ruzesky: the interview is a blend of two conversations which took place at P.K. Page's home in Victoria, B.C. in the summer of 1996 and the fall of 1999. A version of this interview appears in a new collection of writings on and about P.K. Page from Guernica.

Libby Scheier interviewed by Beverley Daurio: the interview was originally published in *Poetry Canada Review*.

Anne Szumigalski interviewed by John Livingstone Clark: the interview was conducted October 10th, 1991.

Fred Wah interviewed by Lola Lemire Tostevin: the interview was originally published in *Poetry Canada Review* and reprinted in *Subject to Criticism*.

Phyllis Webb interviewed by Smaro Kamboureli: this interview took place on Salt Spring Island in the summer of 1991, and was first published in *West Coast Line* 25:3.

Please note that every attempt has been made to acquire permission for reproduction of the material in this book.